Education

Editor: Tracy Biram

Volume 353

ALIS
1776779

Independence Educational Publishers

First published by Independence Educational Publishers

The Studio, High Green

Great Shelford

Cambridge CB22 5EG

England

© Independence 2019

Copyright

Photocopy licence

ISBN-13: 978 1 86168809 5

Printed in Great Britain

Zenith Print Group

Contents

Introduction

EDUCATION is Volume 353 in the *ISSUES* series. The aim of the series is to offer current, diverse information about important issues in our world, from a UK perspective.

ABOUT EDUCATION

With student numbers rising and budgets falling, education in the UK has never been more of an important topic than it is today. In this book we explore some of the issues that affect the education system, and look at ways those issues can be resolved. It also gives an overview of the UK's education up to A-Levels.

OUR SOURCES

Titles in the *ISSUES* series are designed to function as educational resource books, providing a balanced overview of a specific subject.

The information in our books is comprised of facts, articles and opinions from many different sources, including:

◆ Newspaper reports and opinion pieces

◆ Website factsheets

◆ Magazine and journal articles

◆ Statistics and surveys

◆ Government reports

◆ Literature from special interest groups.

A NOTE ON CRITICAL EVALUATION

Because the information reprinted here is from a number of different sources, readers should bear in mind the origin of the text and whether the source is likely to have a particular bias when presenting information (or when conducting their research). It is hoped that, as you read about the many aspects of the issues explored in this book, you will critically evaluate the information presented.

It is important that you decide whether you are being presented with facts or opinions. Does the writer give a biased or unbiased report? If an opinion is being expressed, do you agree with the writer? Is there potential bias to the 'facts' or statistics behind an article?

ASSIGNMENTS

In the back of this book, you will find a selection of assignments designed to help you engage with the articles you have been reading and to explore your own opinions. Some tasks will take longer than others and there is a mixture of design, writing and research-based activities that you can complete alone or in a group.

FURTHER RESEARCH

At the end of each article we have listed its source and a website that you can visit if you would like to conduct your own research. Please remember to critically evaluate any sources that you consult and consider whether the information you are viewing is accurate and unbiased.

Useful Websites

www.cam.ac.uk

www.childlawadvice.org.uk

www.childrenssociety.org.uk

www.daynurseries.co.uk

www.exeter.ac.uk

www.fleet-tutors.co.uk

www.fullfact.org

www.gov.uk

www.impacttutors.co.uk

www.independent.co.uk

www.inews.co.uk

www.junomagazine.com

www.otherwise.education

www.schoolsweek.co.uk

www.shoutoutuk.org

www.strategyeducation.co.uk

www.suttontrust.com

www.telegraph.co.uk

www.theconversation.com

www.theguardian.com

www.theylj.co.uk

What is compulsory school age?

By Matt Hupfield

Compulsory school age refers to the ages at which a child must be in full-time education, usually at a school. The term compulsory school age is slightly confusing as education is compulsory but children do not actually have to go to school.

What is the compulsory school starting age?

Compulsory school starting age is the age at which a child must start full-time education. The Education Act 1996, Section 8, says the following:

A person begins to be of compulsory school age –

◆ (a) when he attains the age of five, if he attains that age on a prescribed day, and

◆ (b) otherwise at the beginning of the prescribed day next following his attaining that age.

What this means is that a child must have started full-time education by the prescribed day after their fifth birthday. The prescribed days are currently 1 September, 1 January and 1 April.

If a child becomes five years old between 1 January and 31 March they are of compulsory school age at the start of the Summer term, after 1 April.

If a child becomes five years old between 1 April and 31 August they are of compulsory school age at the start of the Autumn term, after 1 September.

If a child becomes five years old between 1 September and 31 December they are of compulsory school age at the start of the Spring term, after 1 January.

What is the compulsory school leaving age?

Compulsory school leaving age is the age at which a child can leave full-time education. The Education Act 1996, Section 8, says the following:

A person ceases to be of compulsory school age at the end of the day which is the school leaving date for any calendar year –

◆ (a) if he attains the age of 16 after that day but before the beginning of the school year next following,

◆ (b) if he attains that age on that day, or

◆ (c) (unless paragraph (a) applies) if that day is the school leaving date next following his attaining that age.

In England and Wales, a child can leave school on the last Friday in June (the school leaving date) if they will turn 16 before the end of the summer holidays.

In England a child must then do one of the following until they turn 18 years old:

◆ Remain in full-time education, for example at a school or college.

◆ Start an apprenticeship.

◆ Remain in part-time education or training whilst working or volunteering at least 20 hours per week.

In Scotland, a child who turns 16 between 1 March and 30 September can leave school after 31 May of that academic year. A child who turns 16 between 1 October and the end of February can leave at the start of the Christmas holidays in that school year.

In Northern Ireland a child who turns 16 during the school year (between 1 September and 1 July) can leave school after 30 June. If a child turns 16 between 2 July and 31 August though they cannot leave school until 30 June in the following year.

25 May 2018

www.otherwise.education

Types of school

This article describes the different types of schools in the UK and how they are funded and managed. It explains the difference between maintained schools, academies, free schools and independent schools.

All children in England between the ages of 5 and 16 are entitled to a free place at a state school

What is compulsory school age?

Compulsory education in England and Wales is provided for children between the ages of 5 and 16.

- Primary education is for children from the ages of 5 to 11
- Secondary education is for children from the ages of 11 to 16

There are a few areas of the country which have primary schools for ages 5 to 9, middle schools for ages 9 to 13 and high schools for ages 13 to 16. Some secondary schools also have sixth forms to educate pupils from 16 to 18. Other post-16 options are sixth-form colleges and colleges of further education.

What is a Maintained School?

- These are wholly owned and maintained by local authorities
- They are likely to have a strong link with the local community and often provide services such as childcare, use of their facilities and adult learning classes
- These schools must follow the national curriculum
- There are four main types of maintained schools: community schools, Foundation and trust schools, voluntary aided schools and voluntary controlled schools
- A maintained school can be named in a statement of Special Educational Needs (issued before 1 September 2014) or in an Education, Health and Care Plan (issued after 1 September 2014), after prior consultation with the local authority
- Maintained schools must act in accordance with the Government guidelines on admissions, exclusions and SEN provision

The four main types of maintained schools all receive funding from the local a uthority

What is a Community School?

- Controlled and run by the local authority
- The local authority owns the land and buildings
- The Local Authority determines the admission arrangements

What is a Foundation School?

- Foundation schools are funded by the local authority, but are run by the school governing body
- The governing body is the admission authority for these schools

- The governing body employs the school staff and has primary responsibility for admissions
- The school land and buildings are owned by the governing body or a charitable foundation

What is a Trust School?

- A type of Foundation school which forms a charitable trust with an outside partner; usually a business or a charity
- The decision to become a Trust school is taken by the governing body with parents also having a say
- Similar to a Voluntary Aided school, however, the land is owned by a trust which may include commercial organisations
- Trust schools are run by their governing body

What is a Voluntary Aided School?

- These are usually religious or 'faith' schools, although anyone can apply for a place for their child
- Both the local authority and the supporting body (e.g. the Roman Catholic church) will contribute to the funding of the school
- The governing body employs staff and decides admission arrangements
- The land and buildings are normally owned by a charitable foundation
- The governing body contributes to building and maintenance costs

What is a Voluntary Controlled School?

- Voluntary controlled schools are similar to voluntary aided schools, although these schools are funded solely by the local authority
- The local authority is the admission authority but will consult with the supporting body in drawing up the admission policy
- The land and buildings are usually owned by a charitable foundation
- The local education authority employs the school staff and has responsibility for admissions

What is an Academy?

- Academies are schools that are state funded and free to students but they have much more independence than most other schools, including the power to direct their own curriculum. (This can include the introduction of faith-based topics, or a change to the school hours for example.)

- Academies are defined in section 1A of the Academies Act 2010

- Academies are established by sponsors from business, faith or voluntary groups in partnership with the Department for Education working with the community. Together these fund the land and buildings with the Government covering the running costs

- Academies can be flexible with their curriculum, term dates and staffing to meet local needs

- The provision governing academies is the individual contract (Education Funding Agreement) between the Department of Education (The Education & Skills Funding Agency) and the school

- Most Academies have to follow the same rules regarding admissions, exclusions and special educational needs as maintained schools, but it is advisable to check the Academy's individual Education Funding Agreement. You can find the Academy's Education Funding Agreement on their individual school website page

- The Academy Trust is the admission authority

- An Academy can be named in a statement of Special Educational Needs (issued before 1 September 2014) or in an Education, Health and Care Plan (issued after 1 September 2014), after prior consultation with the local authority

- City academies are academies set up in inner cities and are designed to improve the performance of schools in deprived areas

What is a Free School?

- A free school is a type of Academy

- Free schools are funded by the Government, but are not controlled by the local authority

- Teachers, parents, existing schools, educational charities, universities, or community groups can set up free schools

- The group must form a company and choose members and directors to run it

- These schools have a funding agreement with the Department of Education (The Education Skills Funding Agency). You can find the Academy's Education Funding Agreement on their individual school website page.

- Academies can be flexible with their curriculum, term dates and staffing to meet local needs

Schools specialising in a particular subject

- Though Specialist Schools follow the national curriculum, they can focus on a particular subject area

- Any state secondary school in England (maintained or Academy) can become a specialist school in areas such as technology, language, sports or arts

- The schools must meet full national curriculum requirements but have a special focus on the chosen specialist area

What is a Faith School?

- These are schools with a religious character

- Any new faith schools must have the agreement of parents and the local community, and be approved by the local authority

- Faith schools are usually voluntary controlled

- Voluntary aided faith schools are responsible for setting their own admission policies and teach religious education according to its religious precepts

- Faith schools admit pupils on religious affiliation grounds but many admit those who are not of the school faith and voluntary aided faith schools have to comply with the school admissions code of practice

What is a Grammar School?

- Grammar schools are similar to foundation schools but are permitted to select pupils by ability

- They are funded by the local authority, but run by the governing body, which acts as admission authority

- Parents apply for school places for their child through the local authority-coordinated admissions scheme, but a place will not be offered unless the pupil achieves a set standard in the 11+ examination administered by the local grammar school consortium

- The result of this test will determine whether they can gain entry to the local grammar school

Schools for children with special educational needs

Some children are unable to attend mainstream schools because they have Special Educational Needs or learning difficulties. Local authorities fund some special schools to meet their needs. The national curriculum will be followed as far as possible to ensure that the pupils receive the fullest possible education regardless of disability, but they can differentiate the curriculum if applicable.

Note: Many special schools are independent schools and are not funded by local authorities.

Section 316 of the Education Act 1996 states that a child with special educational needs should be educated in a mainstream school, unless a parent indicates that they do not want their child educated in a mainstream school, or it is incompatible with the efficient education of the other children

Almost all children at Special Schools either have a Statement of Special Educational Needs (issued before 1 September 2014) or an Education Health and Care Plan (issued after 1 September 2014). Parents can express a preference for the school at the time the statement or plan is finalised. If the school is named in a statement or a plan then the school must admit the pupil

City Technology Colleges

- City technology colleges are funded partly by the Government and partly by independent organisations

- They offer a wide range of vocational qualifications alongside GCSEs and A-levels for pupils aged 11–18

- The governing body will act as the admission authority and create its own admission policy

- Funded directly by the Government and offer a wide range of vocational qualifications alongside A-levels or equivalents

- They teach the national curriculum but focus on vocational subjects such as science, mathematics and technology

- A College can be named in a Statement of Special Educational Needs (issued before 1 September 2014) or in an Education, Health and Care Plan (issued after 1September 2014), after prior consultation with the local authority

Independent Schools

- Independent schools may be described as private or public schools and are funded by the fees paid by the parents of pupils, contributions from supporting bodies and investments. They are not funded or run by central government or a local authority

- Independent schools set their own curriculum but all must be registered with the Department for Education and are regularly inspected by the Independent Schools Inspectorate to ensure that standards are maintained

- Independent schools may provide education for all pupils regardless of ability. Some independent schools select students by ability requiring them to pass an entrance examination or test. Some provide education only for pupils with special educational needs or disabilities

- Parents may apply for admission directly to the school. These schools are not subject to the Government School Code Admissions. A local authority can direct an Independent School to admit a child who has a Statement of Special Educational Needs (issued before 1 September 2014) or an Education, Health and Care Plan (issued after 1 September 2014). Funding for the child's place may need to come from the local authority via a statement or plan. Independent schools have their own exclusion policies and procedures and are not subject to government guidance on exclusion

- Independent schools are not allowed to discriminate against pupils on the ground of their disability. If parents believe there has been discrimination in admission or exclusion arrangements, or any other aspect of the provision of education, they may make a complaint of discrimination to the First-tier Tribunal (SEN and Disability).

- Any other type of dispute with an independent school may be a breach of contract between the school and the parent. Some breaches may be actionable in court

Independent primary schools fall into two main categories:

- Pre-preparatory – Aged 2-7

- Preparatory – Up to 11 or 12.

These primary schools are devoted to preparation for the Common Entrance Examination which is required by many independent secondary schools.

Stages of education

Pre-school education

- Between the ages of 2 and 5 children attend pre-school

- The government provides 15 hours of early years entitlement (free) per week for 38 weeks if the child is over 3 years old

Primary education

The School Admissions Code requires school admission authorities to provide for all children to be admitted to school in the September following their 4th birthday. However, a child is not of compulsory school age until the term following their 5th birthday

- Key stage one – Infants (5-7)

- Key stage two – Juniors (7-11)

Secondary education

- Secondary education is compulsory until the last Friday in June of the year the child turns 16

Raised participation age

- Young people who were born after September 1997 must now stay in some form of education or training until they are 18 years of age

- The following options are:

  - Full-time education at school or college

  - An apprenticeship or traineeship

  - Part-time education or training, as well as being employed, self-employed or volunteering for more than 20 hours a week

What are academies – and what are their pros and cons?

The brainchild of former Labour prime minister Tony Blair and his education advisor, Andrew Adonis, academies were introduced through the Learning and Skills Act 2000 to boost struggling schools in deprived inner-city areas.

Since then, the number of academies has grown dramatically to just under 7,500. Most secondary schools now have academy status, as do just over a quarter of primary schools.

Even so, academies continue to come under attack from critics. So what are they – and what are their pros and cons?

So, what exactly are academies?

In the English education system, academies are independent schools which get their funding directly from the Government, rather than their local council.

Unlike traditional state schools, they can set their own term times and do not have to follow the national curriculum. This is on condition that the curriculum is 'balanced and broadly based' and includes English, mathematics and science.

However, they still have to follow the same rules on admissions, special educational needs and exclusions.

Academies are run by individual charitable bodies called academy trusts, which employ the staff.

An academy trust that runs more than one academy is called an academy chain. Roughly two-thirds of academies are in academy chains run by multi-academy trusts.

Are there different types of academies?

Academies fall into two main groups: sponsored academies and converter academies.

Sponsored academies have sponsors such as businesses, faith communities, universities, other schools or voluntary groups, who have majority control of the academy trust. Most of these used to be under-performing schools that became academies to improve their performance.

Converter academies are schools which are deemed successful enough to convert to academies in order to benefit from increased autonomy.

They were introduced in July 2010 as part of the Academies Act. Today, the programme has broadened to include primary and secondary schools, special schools, free schools, university technical colleges (UTCs) and studio schools.

In the English education system, academies are independent schools which get their funding direct from the Government, rather than their local council.

Sponsored academies perform worse than the local authority average
Progress scores for reading, writing and maths for different school types

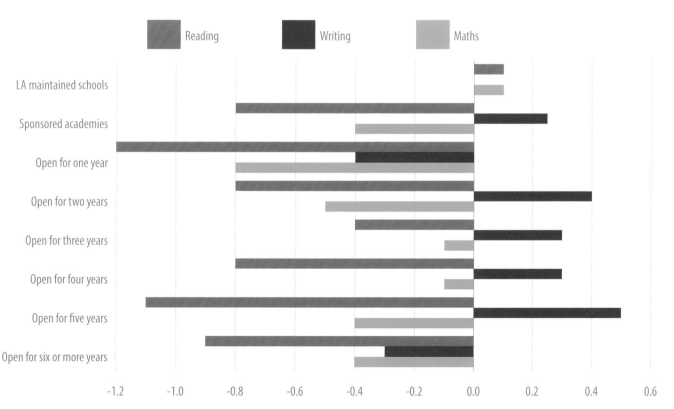

Data: The Department for Education

In the English education system, academies are independent schools which get their funding direct from the Government, rather than their local council

What are the advantages of academy schools?

Supporters of academies argue that they fill the gaps in areas where there are not enough school places for every child and drive up educational standards in disadvantaged areas.

For many, the attraction is the autonomy that academy status brings. In particular, the freedom over budget means more control over where money is allocated in the school – such as salaries and curriculum.

It is also argued that academy status makes it easier to put in place better teaching, leadership, curriculums and accountability, leading to better standards.

What about the cons?

Academies have faced heavy criticism from some teachers, parents and politicians. They see the schools as a move towards privatisation, a waste of money, selective and damaging to existing schools around them.

While freedom from the national curriculum can be seen as a plus, critics claim it gives free rein to religious sponsors to teach topics such as creationism over biology.

Concern has also been raised over staff salaries. The directors of several academy trusts were found to be earning more than some of the UK's best-paid university vice-chancellors. Of the 117 academy trust heads paid more than £150,000 last year, 18 have now agreed to pay cuts.

Have academies been successful?

Evidence on the performance of academies compared to local authority schools is mixed.

Although a number of academies have done well, several have failed to thrive. Some have been placed in special measures.

In 2017, research by the Education Policy Institute found turning schools into academies doesn't automatically improve standards, with the lowest performing primary and secondary schools in academy groups.

The league table also showed there is a larger number of local authorities in the highest performing groups of schools compared to academy chains with seven local authorities in the top ten for primary and secondary schools.

More recently, a Public Accounts Committee (PAC) report said that local authorities' ability to fulfil their statutory responsibilities, including their duty to provide school places, was 'undermined' in areas where a high proportion of schools have become academies.

'Regardless of the extent of academisation, local authorities still retain important statutory responsibilities, including a duty to ensure there are enough school places for local children,' the report said.

'However, they have no control over the number of places in academy schools. There can be particular challenges in finding appropriate places for looked-after children.'

The report also criticised the Department for Education's (DfE) failure to prevent a 'succession of high-profile academy failures', which have been both costly to the taxpayer and damaging to children's education.

13 August 2018

On the way to school: Richard Brinton reflects on school starting age

It was always a very touching moment with our children when, tender little hand holding big hand, we went with each for their first day of school, excitement mixing with varying doses of trepidation on both parts, bigger hand though trying to exude confidence and calm.

When is the right time for our children to start school? And what should they be doing before then? These concerns have never been as contentious as in our current time, and there are conflicting messages coming from different quarters.

On the one hand, there is a relentless push to do things earlier and earlier in schools and nurseries, with the 'schoolification' of early childhood.

On the other hand, ask the British public when they would prefer their children to start school, and one poll suggests that more than two-thirds would prefer at age 6 or 7, in contrast to the actual starting age of 4 to 5 in state schools. Many parents feel that children are under too much pressure at this early age. Is it just arbitrary that 88% of countries start schooling two years later? Or is there something behind this that we can learn from?

A Swiss experience

We often used to go to Switzerland in summer, my wife being Swiss. Some years ago, when our children – who numbered three at the time – were all under 7, we stopped in a village outside Basel, heading for a café with a spacious outdoor area so that the young ones could play.

Being with children is often a conversation opener with strangers, and the impassioned topic that arose with a mother of a young child next to us was… school readiness! 'I hear that Mr X (a politician) is pushing for more learning of the three Rs in kindergarten in Switzerland,' I ventured, curious to hear her view.

'Oh, no, that's not good at all! That's the time they should be playing – that's how they learn at that age!' she replied. I was impressed. Her children went to a local state nursery, yet she was absolutely convinced that formal teaching before age 7 was the wrong approach. But this was Switzerland, and this approach is embedded in the culture and the people. Are they disadvantaged? Along with many other countries where school starts at age 7, Switzerland ranks high in literacy and numeracy, and high in the UN surveys on childhood happiness and wellbeing.

Stepping out of a mindset

We need thus to first realise that our thinking on the issue of school starting age may be strongly influenced by the culture we have grown up in. It can be very instructive to step back and objectively consider the customs of other countries and cultures. What is very interesting is that the 12% of countries where children start school at age 4 or 5 were all once part of the British Empire!

The laws of previous centuries governing an age-7 school start had their roots in deeper-seated customs and wisdom going back to before Roman times: seven-year rhythms were observed in child development, and the first seven years were recognised as a time for play, not for schooling. Notable educators and psychologists of the past two centuries began to examine this further, from Fröbel to Steiner, Piaget, Montessori and more; following more exact scientific observations, all came to the same conclusion – that children benefited most if their activity in the first seven years was based on play, surrounded by the love of adults.

What is happening in the first seven years? Educators and scientists have approached this from different angles, and these are coming together to form a picture of early childhood.

Nurturing natural learning rhythms in life

In the Steiner schools, where I have had involvement, it is acknowledged that the development of the human being is not just physiological: that we need also to nurture the soul forces in the growing child – that each child is a spiritual entity, not just a mass of coincidental atoms. But these soul forces also need time for growing, and, as with all life processes, this happens in certain rhythms. These rhythms are the basis of the seven-year patterns we observe throughout life, especially in the first three periods.

Though the picture is more complex, with intertwining rhythms from other processes, the general observation is of the will life being the predominant force in the first seven years: the grasping of the world through imitation and active interaction. We can easily observe this in the incessant desire of the child for action and doing! The integration of all the senses is very important in this process.

During the second 7-year period, it is especially important to nurture the feeling life, which is why the Steiner school curriculum for this time emphasises the arts and experiential activities, which are integrated into all areas of learning. The arts help the child connect inner life with the world around, giving greater meaning and joy for learning.

In the third period, thinking takes on a new form, more pronounced and individualised; hence this is the time for greater specialisation and abstraction. After this three-times-seven-year period, willing, feeling and thinking have matured to the point of childhood being 'complete'. The age of 21 has always been seen as a significant point in adulthood for this reason.

The scientific physiological research does not differ, but it confirms this picture from other vantage points. The physical development of the child up until age 7 lays a new foundation for the whole of life. Science speaks now of 'embodied cognition', where 'learning' is through experiencing first without thinking. It is this physical activity that builds the neural pathways of the brain. Sitting children at desks and making them prematurely use abstract thinking, worse

still accompanied by computer tablets, significantly limits their integrated sense experiences, affecting physiological development and thus future cognitive abilities.

The general principle for all these findings is that if we work with the natural rhythms of growth in childhood, instead of against them, we will enhance not only long-term learning, but also wellbeing and happiness.

A later school start?

There is not a single study to back up long-term benefits for early schooling. In fact, all the research points to the opposite: that an early school start actually harms children's development, with long-term effects on their attitude to learning as well as on their mental health. In studies by the UN, children in the UK rate very low on the tables for happiness. A later start to school, with early years based on play, increases children's positive learning orientation and significantly enhances their emotional resilience. Any academic 'advantage' from an early start disappears by age 11. Furthermore, economically disadvantaged children suffer the most from early schooling.

We might be tempted to think that all we need to do now is re-present the evidence for a later school start in order for politicians to change the law. Yet in 2013, when 130 educators from around the UK wrote an open letter to the Government calling for raising the school starting age, they received a cold shoulder.

A spokesperson for the then education secretary Michael Gove responded: 'These people represent the powerful and badly misguided lobby who are responsible for the devaluation of exams and the culture of low expectations in state schools…'

Most politicians are still too caught up in the Victorian economically based mindset, espousing slogans like 'Bold Beginnings' for 4-year-olds (the title of a recent Ofsted report), sounding more like a military campaign rather than one showing sensitivity for life. They introduce high-stakes testing, getting schools and parents in a frenzy to try and keep up with league tables, and with countries in competition with each other over PISA test results. This attitude is working its way more and more into early years as well. And it all has nothing to do with childhood understanding and wellbeing.

So the onus is on each of us first of all to enlarge our understanding of and appreciation for the special nature and development of childhood, and to trust in our inner intuition when we feel it is wrong to relentlessly pressure our young children.

The next step is to speak with others about this: for example, speak to your child's school about the baseline testing and then actively encourage alternatives, as is already happening with forest schools and kindergartens where children can truly play. Giving moral and financial support for groups campaigning for children's rights is also part of what we can do.

It all does make a difference. Working together for a positive future for our children.

21 February 2019

The above information is reprinted with kind permission from JUNO Publishing Ltd.
Richard Brinton is a former teacher and Principal. Writer and campaigner on issues of parenting and education; editor of *Growing up Healthy in a World of Digital Media*, Interactions, 2019.
© 2019 JUNO Publishing Ltd

www.junomagazine.com

Starting school young can put child wellbeing at risk

New research has shown that the youngest pupils in each school year group could be at risk of worse mental health than their older classmates.

Starting school young is an exciting but sometimes challenging milestone for children and their families. Some children will be nearing their fifth birthday as they enter foundation classes while others will be only just four.

Now, a study led by the University of Exeter Medical School which investigated more than 2,000 children across 80 primary schools in Devon, has found that children who are younger than their peers when they start school are more likely to develop poorer mental health, as rated by parents and teachers.

A higher score a measure of poor mental health would indicate that children are more likely to experience common negative emotions such as worry and fear, they may have poorer relationships with their peers and be more likely to encounter issues with behaviour and concentration.

Overall the effect was small; however, researchers believe the additional stress of keeping up with older peers could prove a 'tipping point' for vulnerable children, such as those with learning difficulties or who were born prematurely.

The research team was supported by the National Institute for Health Research Public Health Research Programme and the Collaboration for Leadership in Applied Health Research and Care South West Peninsula (NIHR PenCLAHRC).

The research, published in the journal *Child Care, Health and Development*, could have implications on parents' decisions on whether to defer their child's school entry for a school year, permissible under guidance introduced in 2014. The findings could also influence how teachers interact with younger children, particularly those with additional complex needs in the class, and on assessments and teaching and support structures within classrooms.

Anna Price, of the University of Exeter Medical School, was motivated to study the issue after home schooling her own April-born son, who has pre-existing learning difficulties, and was not ready to start school aged five. She said: 'Using such a large dataset was a chance to explore what's really happening in practice for children who start school at a young age. We found that children who started younger had slightly worse well-being – however, this effect was very small and unlikely to make a difference for most. The challenge to well-being of being young for your school year might however be one struggle too many for children who face other challenges to their mental health. Our findings can help guide parents and teachers in making decisions that best support the child.'

The researchers also explored the impact of starting school early on the child's happiness levels and behaviour. In contrast to previous research, they found no significant impact on either. The research paper noted that the schools in the study had strong support in place, such as small group learning, which may have helped improve happiness and behaviour overall.

Professor Tamsin Ford, of the University of Exeter Medical School, oversaw the research. Professor Ford, a practising child psychiatrist, said: 'Being relatively younger could be the tipping point for some, but certainly not all, children. For most it would just be something for teachers to be aware of but for children with other needs or who were born prematurely this difference could be significant. Awareness of this issue among teachers and educators means measures can be put in place that could help to mitigate this effect and get the best outcome for children.'

The full paper, 'Examining the psychological and social impact of relative age in primary school children: a cross-sectional survey', is published in the journal *Child Care, Health and Development*. Authors are A. Price, K. Allen, O. C. Ukoumunne, R. Hayes and T. Ford.

22 June 2017

Summer-born children who defer starting school suffer 'negative effect'

Children born in the summer months, who defer starting school by one or two terms, suffer a 'negative effect' from missing out on the extra time at school that their peers are getting.

By Sue Learner

The research by York University and UCL looked at over 400,000 children born in 2000–2001 on the National Pupil Database who attend state schools in England as well as over 7,000 children in the same year from the Millennium Cohort Study.

Researchers compared early versus later entry into reception class and looked at the impact on their cognitive and non-cognitive skills up until age 11. They found that all children benefit from early schooling; however, the average effects are stronger for disadvantaged boys.

Children in England and Wales start school in the September after their fourth birthday, although some parents feel that if their child is born in the summer months, they are not ready for school and apply to defer them so they start in the spring or summer term of reception.

Co-author of the study, Professor Thomas Cornelissen from the Department of Economics at the University of York, said: 'The idea behind deferment by one or two terms is to give the youngest children some time to become more mature and school ready. But it seems that on average the negative effect of losing one term of reception class outweighs the potentially positive effect of deferment, in particular for boys from disadvantaged family backgrounds.

'The school-entry policy that should be recommended based on our results is a uniform school-entry date at the start of the academic year, while allowing deferment in exceptional circumstances. Importantly, this is the policy that most local authorities today have adopted.'

The study revealed that it is boys from disadvantaged backgrounds, who benefit most from early schooling, helping to narrow the skills gap with boys from high socio-economic backgrounds. Researchers found the early schooling improved relationships with teachers, academic interest and disruptive behaviour.

For disadvantaged boys, early schooling boosted test scores in language and numeracy at age five by 16 – 20 %, personal, social, and emotional development at age five by eight per cent, and language and numeracy skills at age seven by about 10%. For boys from high socio-economic backgrounds, many of these effects are close to zero.

Co-author of the study, Professor Christian Dustmann from UCL added: 'An important finding of the study is that the large skills difference between boys from advantaged and disadvantaged family backgrounds can be substantially reduced by early schooling.

'This is in line with findings of higher positive effects for disadvantaged children of early childcare programmes in other countries, such as Germany. On average across all children, an additional term of early schooling boosted age-5 test scores in language and numeracy by 6-10% and age-7 language and numeracy skills by about 2%'.

The Summer Born Campaign believes that a summer-born child should be allowed to start primary school, in reception class, aged five.

26 February 2019

What age should children start sitting exams?

Exams are a source of constant debate among educators, policymakers, and parents. Recently, ministers revealed plans to introduce testing for 4-year-olds in England. The baseline assessments have been widely criticised, but how do you feel about the proposed move? When is the best time to start exams, and is there a right answer to this question?

The baseline tests, which have been outlined by the Government, are designed to provide an indicator of progression, which follows the child throughout the primary school journey. The results of the assessment, which is carried out when the child starts school, will be used to determine the level of development when compared to results obtained at the end of primary school at the age of 11. The findings, according to ministers, would not only measure the child's progression, but also provide a more accurate insight into how well individual schools are performing. The school standards minister, Nick Gibb, described the new test as a 'quick, simple assessment' that would 'capture the progress that children make' and 'provide a fairer measure for school accountability'.

The test has been criticised by many, but what does it actually involve? The Government is proposing a 20-minute assessment, which measures basic literacy, mathematics, communication and language skills. The test would replace the examinations for Year 2 pupils. The Department for Education stressed that children wouldn't have to prepare for the exam, and the material covered would be largely familiar to them.

Although some educators have welcomed the new test as a replacement for exams for 7-year-olds, there are concerns. Chief executive of the Pre-School Learning Alliance, Neil Leitch, said that testing 4-year-olds would put pressure on the children and promote preparatory work and coaching to ensure that children achieved the best results. Mr Leitch said that the test, which is taken on a tablet, won't provide teachers or parents with useful information about the child, and will serve to increase pressure on very young children.

The Government has tried to introduce baseline tests before, but was forced to scrap the measures. The latest attempt has been criticised by the National Education Union. Mary Bousted, joint general secretary, expressed fears that a new test for reception students would result in children with special educational needs and disabilities and those who are very young within the year group 'being labelled as low ability'. Madeleine Holt, from More Than A Score, a group made up of parents, educational experts and teachers, claimed that there is no evidence to support the fact that 4-year-olds can be tested 'reliably'.

On a slightly more positive note for the Government, the deputy general secretary of the National Association of Head Teachers, Nick Brook, said that the right baseline test could 'see a reduction in the volume of high stakes testing in primary'.

There's a great deal of debate surrounding the introduction of new exams and the right age to test children. It seems as though there will never be a solution that pleases everyone, but perhaps the debate in this article has helped you to form an opinion and think about what age you think children should start sitting exams.

5 August 2018

On such a lovely sunny day four year olds would rather play. Doing tests for those of four is such a terrible awful bore. So, please, oh please without delay, do let us out to play!

Parents plan legal action over new tests for four-year-olds

With a protest march next week and plans to take the Government to court, campaigners are making their voices heard.

By Liz Lightfoot

On Thursday next week Kay Tart, from Hitchin in Hertfordshire, will help her daughter Isla dress in the uniform she will wear when she starts school in September. She will make sure the four-year-old's favourite book and soft toy are in her backpack, but they won't be heading to school. They will be joining other parents and children on the 'march of the four-year-olds' to 10 Downing Street, where Isla will get her first taste of democracy.

The children will hand in a 65,000-signature petition against the new 'baseline' tests the government plans for children aged four and five. They will be piloted at hundreds of schools in September ready for their introduction England-wide at the start of the new school year in 2020.

The parents fear the tests in the first six weeks of their children starting school in reception class will disrupt the important settling-in period. The results will be unreliable, they say, and the emphasis on maths and literacy in the reception baseline assessment (RBA), rather than overall child development, will push schools towards a narrower curriculum. The Department for Education has refused to publish sample questions, which are on maths and literacy and likely to involve counting, recognising letters and vocabulary.

Meanwhile, a group of parents is taking advice on whether they can mount a legal challenge to the Government's plans. Lisa Richardson, a solicitor with Irwin Mitchell, says many teachers and education experts have raised concerns. She says: 'My clients' parents are particularly concerned about potential harm it may cause to their children's health, wellbeing and education, and whether it unfairly disadvantages some children, including younger, summer-born children.

'We are therefore investigating whether the DfE has properly recognised this, assessed it and taken it into account in the design of the RBA process.'

Teachers have consistently opposed the introduction of the tests and the National Education Union (NEU) will reaffirm its campaign against them at its annual conference in Liverpool this week.

> *'It horrifies me they are testing and labelling children from such a young age. It's ludicrous.'*

The tests of maths and literacy, which are costing £9.8 million over two years to develop, are meant to provide a 'baseline' so that children's progress can be measured seven years later at the age of 11 in order to judge schools' effectiveness and hold them to account. Children will be taken out of class one by one to sit the 20-minute test on a tablet operated by the teacher, who will mark questions 'Yes' or 'No'. An algorithm will make the questions easier or harder until it reaches the level at which the children get more wrong than right.

The parents say their children are too young to be tested on numeracy and literacy. 'I've got a four-year-old, and you can ask them what's one plus one and they might say two, or they might say bananas,' says Vicky Trainer from Brighton.

There are also concerns about children being branded by a score so early in their lives, before their brains have fully developed, and about the length of time the children will be taught by people they do not know while their teacher is out testing each pupil individually.

The march is being organised by the campaign group More Than a Score, a coalition of parents and educationists. Tart, who is a member of the group, has five children aged two to nine and says she knows how important the first weeks of reception class are for building a child's confidence and relationships with the teacher and other pupils.

'It horrifies me they are testing and labelling children from such a young age. It's ludicrous, not least because the tests won't achieve any reliable results even if they can get four-year-olds to maintain focus for that long,' says Tart, who worked for a social enterprise helping people into work before starting her family.

Colin, her husband, head of creative design at a retail manufacturer, says he wants his daughter to enjoy her time in reception, especially when she is settling in. 'I don't think that putting children through formal testing at such a young age is a good idea,' he says, 'especially when early-years education is supposed to be about learning through play. It goes against everything we tell our children about starting school and could affect her feelings about education right from the start. It's completely wrong.'

The test scores will not be given to the teachers to help children make progress, but will be held centrally with each child becoming a unique number on a national database. And that worries early childhood education expert Guy Roberts-Holmes of University College London's Institute of Education. He says: 'The Government is testing parents and carers, not schools and teachers, because the children will have just started school. They are formalising school learning as soon as possible. By focusing solely on formal national standardised prescribed numeracy and literacy outcomes, the tests are telling parents that this is what really counts from day one and it is your responsibility as a parent to make sure your child is successful.

'If your child is summer-born or a late developer or has some special educational need or speaks English as an additional language and gets, "No, no, no" answers, then the programme will push the child down to lower-level questions and they will potentially be labelled as having problems. Unfortunately all the evidence suggests that low expectations early on can lead to self-fulfilling prophecies later on.'

Gemma Haley, from Brighton, who is a prospect development manager at the Alzheimer's Society, will be on the march with her son Alex, five, who started school last September. 'Aside from the question of whether it is morally right to test four-year-olds, there is the question of whether the results will have any reliability,' she says. 'I am not against assessment but it should be appropriate and we should be trusting the teachers to assess the things that matter because that is what they are trained to do.'

Experts in assessment claim the questions – designed by the National Foundation for Educational Research – are measuring the wrong things. 'They are assessing maths and literacy when we know from research that these are poor indicators and not what matters for children of this age,' says Jan Dubiel, the national director of Early Excellence, the organisation specialising in early years teaching. 'We should be looking at language skills, how they interact with other children, how they negotiate and share, how they make friendships and resolve disputes.'

A DfE spokeswoman said: 'The RBA will help to provide a starting point to measure how well the school supports children to succeed. There is no pass mark, it is a short, interactive assessment that will help teachers understand how best to support children. Many schools already carry out assessments like this. The data will be used only to form the progress measure. No numerical score will be shared and the RBA will not be used to label or track individual children or to hold early-years providers to account.'

16 April 2019

Is your child studying for GCSEs?

I f so, or if they will in the future, we want you to be aware that GCSEs in England are changing – this started with English and maths in 2017. The reforms ensure that young people have the knowledge and skills they need to succeed in the 21st Century. The new GCSEs ensure that students leave school better prepared for work or further study. They cover more challenging content and are designed to match standards in high performing education systems elsewhere in the world.

Top facts about the new GCSEs

1. The new GCSEs in England have a 9 to 1 grading scale, to better differentiate between the highest performing students and distinguish clearly between the old and new qualifications.

2. Grade 9 is the highest grade and will be awarded to fewer students than the old A*.

3. The first exams in new GCSEs for English language, English literature and maths were sat in summer 2017 and the rest of the new GCSEs will be introduced over the following three years to 2020.

4. The old and new GCSE grading scales do not directly compare but there are three points where they align, as the diagram shows:

   • The bottom of grade 7 is aligned with the bottom of grade A;

   • The bottom of grade 4 is aligned with the bottom of grade C; and

   • The bottom of grade 1 is aligned with the bottom of grade G.

5. Although the exams will cover more challenging content, students will not be disadvantaged by being the first to sit the new GCSEs. The approach used by Ofqual, the qualifications regulator in England, ensures that, all things being equal, broadly the same proportion of students will get grades 1, 4 and 7 and above in the reformed subjects, as would have got G, C or A and above in the old system.

6. The Department for Education recognises grade 4 and above as a 'standard pass' in all subjects. A grade 4 or above marks a similar achievement to the old grade C or above. It is a credible achievement for a young person that should be valued as a passport to future study and employment. A grade 4 is the minimum level that students need to reach in English and maths, otherwise they need to continue to study these subjects as part of their post-16 education. This requirement does not apply to other subjects.

7. Employers, universities and colleges will continue to set the GCSE grades they require for entry to employment or further study. We are saying to them that if they previously set grade C as their minimum requirement, then the nearest equivalent is grade 4. The old A* to G grades will remain valid for future employment or study.

GCSE grading

New grading structure	Old grading structure
9	A*
8	
7	A
6	B
5	
4 Standard pass	C
3	D
2	E
	F
1	G
U	U

When is this happening?

◆ The first exams for new GCSEs in English language, English literature and maths were sat in 2017. An additional 20 new GCSE subjects will have their first exams in 2018.

◆ All GCSE subjects will be revised for courses starting by 2018 and examined by 2020.

◆ Between 2017 and 2019, GCSE exam certificates may have a combination of number and letter grades, depending on the mix of subjects taken. By 2020, all exam certificates will contain only number grades.

May 2018

Why I no longer care about getting the top GCSE grades

In a classroom which is more exam-driven than ever, is it right that children and teachers should have to bear negative consequences?

By Alexander Barrington Brown

Next summer, the same as every year, thousands of students across the country will be taking their GCSEs in sweaty exam halls from Edinburgh to Exeter. For a few weeks students write on pages which will determine their A-levels, careers and, to a certain degree, success for years to come. As a nation we put immense pressure on 16-year-olds to succeed in these exams. With new reforms, however, which have been falling into place over the past few years, this becomes a more challenging goal. Exam stress is becoming more common among teens and is a huge issue for schools and parents, with its root cause being the more pressurised and exam-focussed classrooms.

What's changed?

I first want to start by informing the readers who have previously sat their GCSEs about the recent changes. The whole grading system has changed from the A*–G system to the numerical 9–1 boundaries; with 9 being the equivalent of a high A* and 1 being the equivalent of a G. Furthermore, much of the coursework section has been dropped and exams are taken at the end of the two-year study period in comparison to end-of-module assessments. Content is also deemed to be more challenging with more substantial texts in English Literature and two new topics in Maths, as an example.

A botched curriculum

The first point I wish to make in relation to the title of this article is that I personally don't believe that what the GCSE syllabus teaches is good preparation for life. It's not to say that what is taught is not useful, interesting or practical. But the way in which students are meant to learn is neither interesting, useful, nor thought-provoking. GCSE exams favour and reward the regurgitation of knowledge, they fail to encompass creativity or free thinking.

For example, English Literature; an exam which, at first glance, would suggest deep thought and personal ideas. But for GCSE however, if good grades are what the candidate wishes to achieve, their creativity and free thinking is cut to be replaced by the regurgitation of previously formulated ideas and quotations which have been meticulously analysed and memorised prior to the exam. This shouldn't be the way in which children get through education – all drilled into the same uninteresting mould with a significant lack of room for individuality, creativity or expression.

Thinking backwards

The new purely knowledge-based exam system is, for the most part, completely useless for anything besides GCSEs.

Children should be taught to understand the content in front of them and question its relevance and credibility, rather than simply know what it is. More interestingly, the so-called 'new' system is not really new at all. It harks back to the days of O-levels 30 years ago, that rewarded knowledge and knowledge alone; and so was changed for the better in 1988. Just because the exams are easy – supposedly the problems with the old GCSEs – that is not necessarily a bad thing as long as students gain a passion for learning. There is certainly a reason why Finland is so often praised for its education system, as it doesn't put pressure on students with exams but instead fosters their thoughts, creating some of the most intelligent and well-educated people anywhere in the world.

Achieving a 9 in misery

Additionally, GCSEs have posed significant mental health problems for myself and a number of my peers. A friend of mine for example, missed almost 14 months of school, which then extended into his first year of A-levels. This depressive episode was caused by enormous exam pressure placed upon him by his school: *'I felt swamped, like there was no escape from it'*, he stated.

Another has been in school intermittently somewhat due to the overbearing nature of the GCSE course: *'It evokes no joy…everything is the same, there is no life to anything'*.

I myself experienced occasional periods of anxiety and sorrow due to the pressure brought upon by my GCSE course. Being constantly surrounded by accounts of people achieving top grades, it is demoralising and humiliating to some that they are told on a constant basis simply to achieve, not to be creative or express their ideas but to get grades and grades alone.

An unhappy correlation

Is it really right that as a society we can allow young teenagers to be degraded to the point of depression, self-harm and in some cases suicide? ChildLine processes thousands of calls from people under 19, many of which are about exam stress. In the 2016/2017 exam period it delivered over 3,000 counselling sessions about exam stress – this is a 2% increase from the previous year and an 11% increase from just two years prior. The spike plausibly correlates with the new GCSE formulation, and although other factors may be present, the correlation has to be recognised.

A similar charity, Young Minds, published its counselling statistics showing that almost 40% of its counselling sessions were related to exam stress. Furthermore, stress and anxiety is not just something which charities have to deal with, teachers too now have to delve into the realm of emotional support. 78% of teachers stated that they had observed increased levels of stress last year, as compared to the previous year, according to the NSPCC. Suicide rates among young people have also seen exponential rises of 67 per cent since 2010. Lucie Russel of the charity stated that: *'For a child who has problems in other areas of their life, such as family breakdown or friendship issues, exams can be the "last straw".'*

Take action!

So as your teachers continue to drill in knowledge which a day after your exam will be completely defunct. Be the change: Write to the Department of Education, do what you can to fight for a GCSE which works for all. But remember, don't overstress. The world will still turn if you do not get that grade 9, as I have come to find out. That's why I no longer care about achieving the top GCSE grades.

GCSE results: boys drive slightly improved performance

This year's GCSE results were released today. Overall, there has been a slight pick-up in performance levels, after a couple of years of decline, in pupils achieving higher grades.

However, as with our assessment of last week's A-level results, it's important to remember that any reported changes are likely to be much less dramatic than they sound.

A rise in, say, the number of pupils achieving top grades, is likely to be a matter of a few percentage points. Changes in performance also need to be taken in a longer term context to be properly understood, not looked at compared to last year in isolation.

Those warnings aside, there are a couple of interesting trends to note. A pick up in overall achievement of grade A/7 and above, or C/4 and above (we'll explain the new grading system in a moment) is driven by boys in particular. They've shown a slight increase in achievement of these grades, while achievement among girls is much the same as in previous years.

Some of the biggest declines in performance are in Wales – which has seen a five percentage point drop in achievement of grade C/4 over the past two years.

The data analysed in this article all comes from the FFT Education Datalab, and covers England, Wales, and Northern Ireland (most students in Scotland don't sit GCSEs).

What's happened to the grading system?

20 subjects in England and Wales, were assessed based on a new format this year. Three subjects: English, Maths and Welsh, already made the switch last year.

The new format is mainly assessed by exam, with a reduced amount of coursework. Courses are no longer divided into modules, and students take all their exams in one period at the end of the course. It's also designed to include 'new, more demanding content'.

A new grading system has been introduced for the new format of assessment (from 9 to 1, instead of A* to G), which is designed to 'allow greater differentiation between students'. Grades 7–9 are equivalent to the old A–A*, while 4–6 equates to C–B.

Ofqual—the body that regulates examinations in England—has previously said that the distribution of grades should be broadly the same under the new grading system. It uses predictions based on students' prior attainment to ensure this.

Overall performance

This year has seen an increase of about half a percentage point in the level of students in England, Wales and Northern Ireland achieving grade A/7 or above, and C/4 or above.

This represents a slight pick-up in performance, after a decline in the previous two years. A/7 achievement fell by around one percentage point from 2015 to 2017, while C/4 achievement fell by about three percentage points.

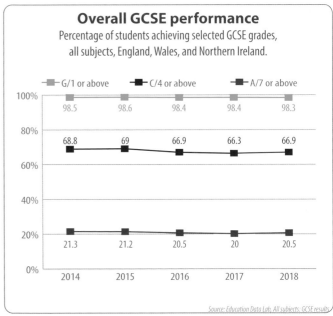

Overall GCSE performance
Percentage of students achieving selected GCSE grades, all subjects, England, Wales, and Northern Ireland.

G/1 or above   C/4 or above   A/7 or above

	2014	2015	2016	2017	2018
G/1 or above	98.5	98.6	98.4	98.4	98.3
C/4 or above	68.8	69	66.9	66.3	66.9
A/7 or above	21.3	21.2	20.5	20	20.5

Source: Education Data Lab, All subjects, GCSE results

Performance among boys has picked up this year

Overall, girls continue to perform better than boys, particularly at the higher grade levels.

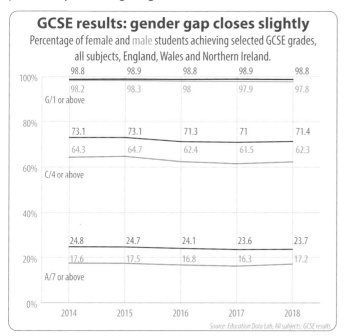

GCSE results: gender gap closes slightly
Percentage of female and male students achieving selected GCSE grades, all subjects, England, Wales and Northern Ireland.

	2014	2015	2016	2017	2018
G/1 or above	98.8 / 98.2	98.9 / 98.3	98.8 / 98	98.9 / 97.9	98.8 / 97.8
C/4 or above	73.1 / 64.3	73.1 / 64.7	71.3 / 62.4	71 / 61.5	71.4 / 62.3
A/7 or above	24.8 / 17.6	24.7 / 17.5	24.1 / 16.8	23.6 / 16.3	23.7 / 17.2

Source: Education Data Lab, All subjects: GCSE results

But performance amongst boys has picked up notably this year, after a couple of years of decline. Both boys and girls saw dips in the proportion achieving grade A/7 or above from 2015 to 2017 (by around one percentage point each). Since then girls' performance has stabilised while boys' performance is up by around one percentage point.

It's a similar story at grade C/4 or above. After a drop of around three percentage points from 2015 to 2017, boys' performance picked up by around one percentage point this year. Girls saw a smaller version of the same trend: the drop was about two percentage points from 2015 to 2017, followed by a rise of about half a percentage point.

A tale of two regions

Performance across the different regions in the UK is where we see some of the biggest fluctuations this year. Overall, Northern Ireland continues to significantly outperform England and Wales.

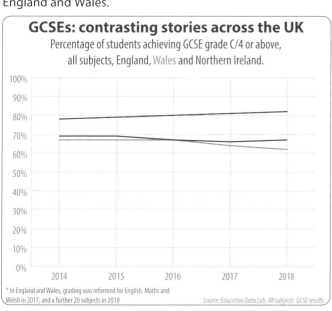

GCSEs: contrasting stories across the UK
Percentage of students achieving GCSE grade C/4 or above, all subjects, England, Wales and Northern Ireland.

In England and Wales, grading was reformed for English, Maths and Welsh in 2017, and a further 20 subjects in 2018

Source: Education Data Lab, All subjects: GCSE results

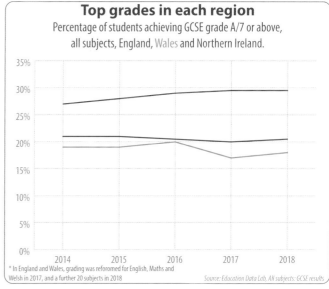

Top grades in each region
Percentage of students achieving GCSE grade A/7 or above, all subjects, England, Wales and Northern Ireland.

In England and Wales, grading was reformed for English, Maths and Welsh in 2017, and a further 20 subjects in 2018

Source: Education Data Lab, All subjects: GCSE results

The difference is most stark among students achieving grade C/4 or above. The level rose by about one and a half percentage points in Northern Ireland, half a percentage point in England, and it fell by just over one percentage point in Wales. The drop in performance in Wales is most notable—the 1.2 percentage point fall this year follows a 3.8 percentage point fall the year before. England sees a pick-up of 0.5 percentage points, after falling almost three percentage points in the previous two years.

There's better news for Wales in terms of performance at the very highest grades. Achievement of grade A/7 or above rose by about half a percentage point this year, after a fall of one and a half percentage points the year before (it was pretty flat prior to this). England saw a rise of half a percentage point after a few years of decline, while Northern Ireland stayed broadly flat after a few years of slight increases.

23 August 2018

Do A-level results matter or not? A question for our unscrupulous universities

Universities have merrily sacrificed academic standards on the altar of cash. The school sector should not let them forget that.

By Laura McInerney

If you're the parent of an 18-year-old, it is time to pat yourself on the back. The country has a shortage of this age group, due to a birth dip at the time of the millennium. Not only does this mean the group will have an incredible market value in a few years' time when graduate recruiters struggle to fill their vacancies; this little cohort has also done us a massive favour and shown just how unscrupulous our university sector can be.

Back in 2015, I wrote about the sharp increase in unconditional offers given to A-level students. So instead of having to strive for top grades, applicants were being accepted on the basis of the grades teachers predicted they would achieve. Although this sounds positive, the offers often came with a requirement for the student to put the university as their first choice, putting pressure on the young person to select a lower-tier university in return for being able to faff about in their summer term rather than revise. It reduces student motivation, which is a nightmare for school leaders who are judged by grades, even if their pupils aren't.

'Last year an outrageous 34% of university place offers were unconditional.'

At the time, my comments were decried by university professionals who said I was over-exaggerating, as the situation was affecting only about 5% of students, that there was no evidence it reduced pupils' grades and there was no reason to believe things would get worse.

Flip forward, and last year an outrageous 34% of university place offers were unconditional, and the university admissions service, UCAS, found that those with unconditional offers were more likely to slip two or more grades. And while the practice is most popular among lower-tariff universities, even some of the so-called elite Russell Group lot have led the way.

Over the years, universities have variously claimed these offers alleviate mental health problems due to exam pressures. Or they somehow help social mobility. But let's get real. The simple reason for the offers is that there aren't as many 18-year-olds as in other cohorts, and with the cap on the number of places they can offer removed, many universities have spent a fortune on building massive new residential halls and expanding their courses. They need as many warm bodies as possible to fill these up or their budgets will be in peril.

Thankfully, the Education Secretary, Damian Hinds, has shown that he can, on occasion, grow a backbone, and has written to the worst offenders urging them to stop. Only

time will tell if he can also grow some teeth and make his words sink in.

That said, he probably won't need to. Over the next eight years, cohort numbers start increasing again so the incentive soon wears off. It's therefore no surprise to hear the University of Nottingham saying it will stop the practice. Indeed, by the time the current surfeit of 10-year-olds are applying for university, the likelihood is there'll be so many we'll be back to the good old days of professors moaning that A-levels don't adequately prepare students for university and that it's impossible to choose from among the zillions of A grades. Except we can all laugh knowing those voices are in the key of hypocrisy singing verses of bullshit. When it suited, universities merrily sacrificed academic standards on the altar of cash. The school sector should not let them forget that.

Ultimately, the university sector needs to decide: do A-level grades matter, or don't they? It is fundamentally unfair to tell one generation it's the only way to select them while telling another that it's a free-for-all. And if you are one of the rare parents of an 18-year-old, I wish you luck this summer in getting them to focus their efforts. On the upside, if they make it through, by the time they reach the graduate market, they will be very valuable indeed.

16 April 2019

GCSE and A-level results: it's not just the grades that matter

An article from The Conversation.

By Jake Anders, Senior Research Fellow in Education, Evaluation and Inequality, Department of Learning and Leadership, UCL Institute of Education, UCL and Catherine Dilnot, Senior Lecturer, Oxford Brookes University

A-level results will soon be out, with more than 300,000 students eagerly waiting to find out if they've made the grade. Then come GCSE results, with even more students keen to find out how they've done.

Whether students are heading to university, into an apprenticeship or straight into employment, chances are they will all be wishing and hoping and dreaming and praying of a set of grades that will reflect their level of academic accomplishment.

For would-be university applicants, there is often a requirement that students take a particular set of subjects at A-level – and achieve a certain grade – to be in with a chance of getting a place on a degree course. To study medicine, for example, it's often required that an applicant has taken chemistry and biology at A-level.

In this way, the subjects a student chooses to study at school can have long-term consequences. In England, young people start making decisions on subject choice at the age of 14 when they pick GCSE options. For many pupils this may seem far too early to be thinking about what they want to do with the rest of their life. So given the fact that many students may not have decided what career path they want to take, are there subjects that are 'better' to study than others?

The current advice

The Russell Group – which is made up of 24 leading UK universities – publishes an annual guide to A-level subject choice for 16-year-olds known as *Informed Choices*. This suggests A-levels in science, maths, languages, history and geography are good choices for students to take if they want to keep their options open.

This is also in part why the English Baccalaureate (EBacc) – which aims to give students a wide background in a variety of subjects at GCSE level – was introduced in 2010. According to the Schools Minister, Nick Gibb, it includes subjects the Russell Group identifies as 'key for university study'. To count towards the EBacc, a pupil must achieve GCSE grade C or above in English, maths, history or geography, two sciences and a language.

With this in mind, our research set out to understand the implications of subject choice and if these choices then play a part in whether students go to university – and where they end up studying.

We looked at the subjects chosen by young people at the age of 14 and 16 and found that pupils who study the full set of EBacc subjects are slightly more likely to go to university than those who don't.

Our research also revealed that studying certain A-level subjects often leads to a place at a better ranked university. So a student who studies some combination of science, maths, languages, history and geography is more likely to attend a higher ranked university, than a student who chooses A-levels outside of these subjects.

Vocational vs traditional

Our research also revealed that studying more vocational subjects at both GCSE and A-level may be less helpful in terms of getting into a higher ranked university. We found that those who studied applied GCSE subjects (which are more vocational) were less likely to attend university.

These vocational-style GCSEs were introduced in 2002 and include subjects such as applied business and applied home economics. But their introduction has since been criticised, as many of the qualifications have been downgraded in performance tables.

There was found to be a similar picture at A-level. Students who studied the more vocational study subjects – such as accounting or business – were more likely to go to a lower ranked university.

The most striking results were in law. Consistent with anecdotal evidence that higher ranking universities 'don't like' law A-level, our research shows that studying law at A-level is associated with attending a lower ranked university. So although a 16-year-old who aspires to have a career in law, accounting or business might think that an A-level directly related to the profession would help them take their chosen path, this may not actually be the case. But whether this is because law A-level is perceived by universities to be an easier A-level, or because those with law A-level are applying to lower ranked universities is unclear.

Either way, what all this shows is that while the subjects young people study in school are important for next steps in education, there are some subjects that can be more important than others in helping to further horizons.

Although that said, it's important to emphasise that the differences are not large. Ultimately, it's far more important to perform well in whatever subject studied. But still, when it comes to students deciding what subjects to choose at A-level or GCSE, it might be worth them trying to keep their options open, where possible.

14 August 2017

What is it like to experience exam stress? A student perspective

By Tamsin McCaldin, Kerry-ann Brown and Dr Jo Greenwood

With recent changes to exams in England, there has been increased media interest into exam stress and what that might mean for students working towards exams. Although it is likely that anyone preparing for and taking exams will experience some stress and anxiety, research has suggested that around 15% of GCSE students may fall into the category of being 'highly test anxious' (Putwain & Daly, 2014). For these students, their levels of stress and anxiety are high enough that their well being and exam performance can be negatively affected.

In response to a growing awareness, many articles have been published giving tips and advice on how to manage and cope with exam stress but little focus has been directed towards what it's like for the students who are actually experiencing exam stress. Here, Jemma and Sami, two GCSE students in Year 11, give an insight into what it's like for them to experience stress around their exams.

These are real accounts from students. Although only two are presented here, these examples illustrate common experiences of many students. They show the importance of listening to students, to gain the insight needed to provide the right support.

What is exam stress like?

For Sami, feeling stressed is what he associates most with the topic of exams. 'The whole time is just a stressful thing,' he says. 'All everyone's talking about is how your exams are

really soon and they're the most important things… it's like the whole world – it's just stress.'

Jemma shares the experience that stress around exams is not confined to the exam itself, or to revision. She explains that she sees the stress as starting early and being everywhere. 'You start to feel it as soon as you're in Year 10 kind of – maybe before actually… And then in Year 11 it's everywhere. Everyone's stressing.'

Sami explains that in certain situations, such as when he's feeling unmotivated to complete a piece of work he knows he's able to do, a small amount of stress can be helpful. 'If I'm stressing over it,' he says, 'I'll be able to get it and do it really quick. Whereas, if I'm not really bothered, like, not really stressed about it, I won't.' Sami's exam stress, however, is different and more extreme. It is unpleasant to experience and something he perceives as having a negative impact on his work. 'Too much stress is just getting you panicked,' he explains. 'And you can't do anything because it's too much.' His only solution to remove the feeling is to 'move away from revision to calm down because you can't do anything like that'.

Jemma's experience of stress is similar. 'The amount of pressure on that high level,' she says, 'is sometimes so overwhelming that you don't want to do it.' Like Sami, she finds herself moving away from exam preparation and revision because of how stressed it makes her feel. She also

describes feeling that stress will affect her during the exam, saying 'who wants to sit there in an exam hall and be, like, doing this test when you can't remember anything because you're that stressed out?'

Both students explain that feeling stressed can make them feel negatively about all aspects of their school and exam work. Jemma explains that, 'feeling that bad makes you feel like nothing's right. Everything's going to go bad.' When she gets extremely stressed she can begin to feel like she won't get the grades she hopes for and describes feeling like she's 'just going to fail, and then there's nowhere else to go'. Being extremely stressed can make the situation seem hopeless and success in their exams seem impossible.

What causes exam stress?

Both Jemma and Sami talk about not knowing what various aspects of the exam will be like, and this element of the unknown being a source of stress.

For Jemma, it is uncertainty around the exam itself which is a source of stress. 'You don't know what it's actually like,' she says, when trying to imagine being in the exam. Even though she has taken mock exams there are still parts of the 'real exams' which remain unknown. 'You don't know the people who give out the papers,' she says, talking about the school's use of independent invigilators, 'or where you're going to be and stuff and that's ominous with stress. It's horrible.'

Sami describes feeling unsure about the questions which will come up in the exams. His teachers, he says, are more focused on teaching the content of the course than the structure of the exam. He describes asking his teacher about sample exam questions, because he feels, 'we need to know what we're going to come up against in the exam'. Sami explains that his teachers, 'say we don't. Like, we don't have to worry about that right now, that's something we do later. I think they will tell us later and that but it's scary not knowing.'

For both students, as well as the unknown aspects of the exam itself, their lack of confidence in revision technique and confusion around what revision should look like was another source of stress.

Sami and Jemma give similar descriptions of their teachers highlighting the importance of revision, and encouraging them to do it. Sami views his teachers as saying, 'you know what, just go home, go revise everything. You've got a test coming up,' but explains that he is left feeling that 'you don't know what that means'. He feels unclear on exactly what he should revise, and how he should go about doing it, stating that he wants his teachers to 'just tell us what we're meant to do'.

Jemma explains how feeling unsure of how to revise causes her stress. 'Me as a person revising is just not good,' she says, 'because, I will stress over it, and I will freak out about it and I just won't remember anything and I'll do crap in the exam.' And why does she see revision as a source of stress? 'Because,' she explains, 'the whole time you're thinking "is this going to be something I remember? Am I doing it right? Should I be reading stuff or making flash cards or something?"'.'

What can teachers do?

Interestingly, both students see their stress as something their teachers don't, and can't understand. 'Unless you've lived with a child who's telling you a lot about their lives and how stressed they are about their GCSEs, you're not going to know what it's like,' explains Sami. 'There's not much connection, to be honest,' Jemma says, talking about how much her teachers can understand about her experience of taking exams. 'The things they say don't even make sense for us. They don't know what we're thinking.' Despite this, they both agree that there are things teachers could do to improve their experience of working towards exams and reduce their stress.

'They should tell us that it's not everything,' says Jemma. 'Because that's what every teacher tells us, that our GCSEs will set the future for all our lives. But it won't. Like, it just won't'. Sami agrees. His maths teacher, he says, already does something like this. 'He says, you know what, if you don't pass your GCSEs, at least you still learnt something and I'd prefer you learnt something than learn nothing and pass your GCSEs.' As well as making the exams seem more manageable, this gives Sami the sense that his teacher's support is not conditional on his exam performance. 'As least I've still got somebody who will be with me,' he says. 'Even if I don't pass my GCSEs, it's somebody who will give me support and guidance, and still be confident in me. Like, who knows that GCSEs are just exams and you might not pass, but you don't fail.'

'Advice on doing revision,' Sami says, is something he and Jemma agree would reduce stress when preparing for exams. 'I think they should give us different types of revision,' Sami continues. 'Like, what we should actually do, not just "go and revise", because there's difference types and one type won't work for everyone. I think it's quite important.' Advice on specific revision techniques would 'make you more confident', Jemma explains, and reduce stress.

Although, Jemma says, 'some kids really want to do well', sshe perceives teachers as 'putting on pressure', telling students they are, or should be, stressed. 'Just be gentler,' is what she advises teachers. 'The pressure is sometimes way too much especially when it comes to revising and studying and extra lessons. Don't tell us we should be stressed. We don't need any more stress.'

As Sami and Jemma's accounts show, students' experiences of exams are complex. Discussing stress with your students can help to understand what they are experiencing. Although there are common reactions to stress, each student's response is likely to be unique. By listening to what they have to say, you can begin to understand how to help and what support and techniques they could be given to empower them to help themselves.

8 March 2019

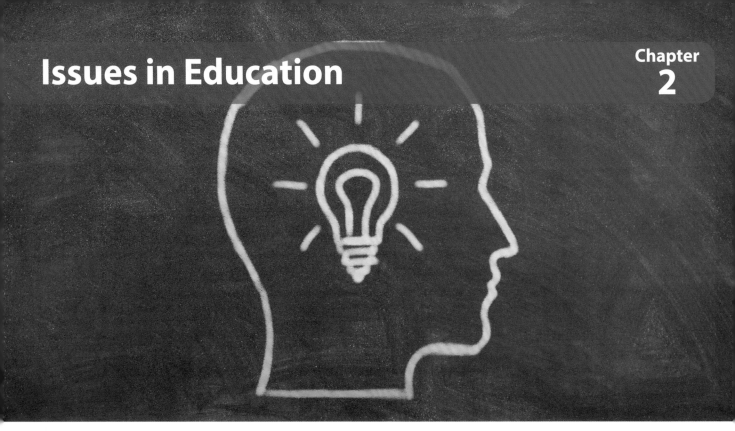

Does poor attendance really have an impact on student learning?

By Claudia Kelly, Education Leader, Fleet Tutors

A register is taken at each and every class a student attends, but does poor attendance really make a difference if a student misses lessons due to a short illness, the dentist or a doctor's appointment? Or even more controversially, a family holiday?

Absence from lessons raises a host of questions including where the responsibility lies between the teaching and learning cycles of activity. Educational institutions, authorities and governments set policies and strategies in an attempt to encourage students to attend throughout each academic year.

But the one question that does not factor in still remains; Does attendance or the lack of – in this case, poor attendance – really have that much of an impact on a student's achievement?

Obviously, a student whom for whatever reason, has long-term absences from classes will eventually lack access to teaching, which invariably has a knock-on effect on their learning. But what about odd days and weeks spread across the academic year? Does that really matter in terms of long-term achievement goals?

In March 2016 the Department for Education (DfE) published a report on the link between absence and attainment in Key Stages 2 and 4. The findings for both Key Stages show that in general, the higher the absence rate, the lower the likely level of attainment. The report states that at Key Stage 2:

'… pupils with no absence are 1.3 times more likely to achieve level 4 or above, and 3.1 times more likely to achieve level 5 or above, than pupils that missed 10 –15 per cent of all sessions.'

At KS4 the study reports that:

'… pupils with no absence are 2.2 times more likely to achieve 5+ GCSEs A*-C or equivalent and 2.8 times more likely to achieve 5+ GCSEs A*– C or equivalent including English and mathematics, than pupils missing 15 – 20% of Key Stage 4 lessons.'

The report also highlights that 73% of pupils who have over 95% attendance achieve five or more GCSEs at grades A*– C and explains that pupils with persistent absences are less likely to attain at school, and – very importantly in terms of the future of the UK workforce – are unlikely stay in education after the age of 16 years.

All this is a fairly well-trodden path for experienced educationalists. However, a report from Warwick University looked into the attendance of economics undergraduates and there were some surprising results. The study found some very expected and stereotypical outcomes which included:

- morning classes have a high rate of absenteeism – especially 9.00am classes

- female students miss fewer classes than male students

- overseas students miss more classes than home (European Union) students.

Interestingly, they also found:

- missing classes has an adverse effect, but only for 'high ability' students, and missing 10% of classes was associated with a 1-2 percentage point lower mark for this group of students

- students who have performed well in their first year tend to have lower absenteeism rates in their second year.

Even accounting for the discrepancy between the two widely differing age groups these last two points seems to present a new twist in the importance of attendance in education. It is very often assumed that more-able students can catch up if they miss lessons and the importance of poor attendance is focused on the less-able students.

This would appear to be too simplistic.

All students need to be reminded of the link between attendance and achievement and the argument that bright students can miss a little time may not, upon closer scrutiny, hold. The point which references student attendance as more likely when the student has performed well in the first year of study is also significant. To conclude that success builds confidence, which leads to a greater commitment to achieve further, would seem to be quite probable.

Still, there are students who struggle to achieve a good attendance record; irrespective of all the research into the importance of attendance, statistical evidence to support the negative impact of missing lessons and numerous institutional initiatives to engage students in their own learning.

This is where classroom teachers and tutors can make a real difference.

Whether you are teaching a class or supporting a student on a one-to-one basis, young people need to know that you really care and believe in their potential for success and achievement. Planning for students' success; delivering interesting, engaging and varied lessons and creating a 'can do' environment, does go a long way towards ensuring students keep turning up.

Coupled with a sympathetic but firm 'nowhere to hide' determination to curb absenteeism, your efforts will eventually pay off – even more so where institutional initiatives may have failed!

29 June 2018

ATTENDANCE...

- IT DOES MAKE A DIFFERENCE!

EDUCATION

Children 'falling off the grid' in the tens of thousands amid surge in pupils leaving mainstream education

Children's Commissioner warns that 60,000 children, many with special educational needs, are permanently out of school as more families feel they have no choice but to home educate.

By May Bulman

The number of children being taken out of school to be home educated has surged in recent years, prompting calls for greater supervision of youngsters not in mainstream education.

The Children's Commissioner warned that 60,000 children, many of whom are vulnerable or have special educational needs, are permanently out of school and therefore effectively 'off the grid'.

Research by Anne Longfield shows the number of children who are known by councils to be home educated was 27 per cent higher in 2018 than in 2017, and has risen by 20 per cent in each of the last five years – doubling since 2013 – 14.

The Commissioner warned that while some parents make an informed decision to home educate and provide their children with a high-quality education, a growing number of families feel they have no choice but to home educate because the school cannot cater for their child, and are struggling without help.

Separate research from a Channel 4 *Dispatches* documentary to be aired on Monday reveals that one in five children withdrawn from school has special educational needs and disabilities (SEND), and that 88 per cent of councils are worried about off-rolling, where schools move difficult-to-teach pupils off the school register to boost performance data.

'Many of these children are very vulnerable, have special educational needs, or are unable to cope with a "one size fits all" school system. Schools should be for all children, including those with complex needs and those who struggle academically,' said Ms Longfield.

'The numbers are rocketing and no one knows how they are doing academically or even if they're safe. Many are being off-rolled. It also seems that a relatively small number of schools may be responsible for this sharp rise in children leaving school for "home education" in this way.'

The report found that some schools were making more than 15 referrals into home education a year. In Hackney, there was a 94 per cent rise in home schooling and in Newham the figure stood at 176 per cent. Between 2016–17 and 2017–18, Hackney's academies saw a 238 per cent increase of children moving into home education.

Local authorities warned in November that vital support for children with SEND was facing a potential funding gap of more than half-a-billion pounds – more than double the gap they faced the previous year.

Ms Longfield added: 'We need to know who these children are, where they are, whether they are safe and if they are getting the education they need to succeed in life. There is a clear case for the Government to introduce a compulsory register for all home-educated children, without delay.'

The findings have prompted calls for local councils to be awarded powers and appropriate funding to enter homes or other premises to ensure children aren't being taught in unsuitable or dangerous environments.

Cllr Anntoinette Bramble, chair of the Local Government Association's Children and Young People Board, said: 'Placing a legal duty on parents to register home-schooled children with their local authority would also help councils to monitor how children are being educated and prevent them from disappearing from the oversight of services designed to keep them safe.'

A Department for Education spokesperson said: 'Unofficial exclusions are illegal regardless of whether they are done with the agreement of parents or carers and regardless of the age of the pupil.

'Where a pupil is asked to leave the school, the formal exclusions process set out in the school exclusion guidance must be followed.

'Where children are being home educated, we know that in the vast majority of cases parents are doing an excellent job.

'We also know, however, that in a very small minority of cases children are not receiving the standard of education they should be, which is why last year we ran a call for evidence on proposals to introduce a register, as well as monitoring of provision and support for home educators. We will respond to that in due course.'

3 February 2019

More than 49,000 pupils 'disappeared' from English schools – study

Data reveals one in 12 schoolchildren in 2012–17 were removed from rolls without explanation.

By Sally Weale

An investigation into the true scale of 'off-rolling' from schools in England has found that more than 49,000 pupils from a single cohort disappeared from the school rolls without explanation.

Researchers from the Education Policy Institute (EPI) said that one in 12 pupils (8.1%) from the national cohort who began secondary school in 2012 and finished in 2017 were removed from rolls at some point, for unknown reasons.

Off-rolling is the practice whereby schools remove difficult or low-achieving pupils from their rolls so that they are not included in their GCSE results, or in order to reduce costs.

Unions said the findings were shocking. Over the five-year period the EPI identified a total of of 55,300 unexplained exits by 49,100 pupils – some of whom will have been moved more than once – and the numbers appear to have gone up in recent years.

For the first time, the research takes into account pupils removed from school rolls due to family reasons, such as moving house, or to a higher-performing school, so the figures represent pupil exits that are likely to have been instigated by schools who may be seeking to improve GCSE results or manage pressures on school budgets.

The research, which claims to be the most comprehensive analysis to date of unexplained pupil exits, also revealed that rates were particularly high in a small number of schools. Just 330 schools, which constitute 6% of secondary schools in England, accounted for almost a quarter (23%) of the total number of unexplained moves in 2017.

According to the EPI, those schools with very high exit rates removed the equivalent of an entire classroom of children from a single year group as they made their way through secondary school between 2012 to 2017.

The EPI's executive chairman, David Laws, commented: 'The size of unexplained pupil moves is disturbing and will raise concerns about whether some schools are "off-rolling"' pupils.'

Some students leave through a 'managed move', when a school finds another institution to take them on, while others are encouraged to be home-educated. Unlike formal exclusions, there is no requirement to record the reason why these pupils have been removed from a school roll. A government review is currently under way looking into exclusions and off-rolling, which is due to report imminently.

Dr Mary Bousted, joint general secretary of the National Education Union (NEU), which sponsored the research, said: 'The data is shocking, if not surprising. There are nearly 55,000 pupils experiencing unexplained moves, but it is specific groups of students experiencing off-rolling at a far greater rate.

'It is urgent that we move beyond the numbers, analyse the real reasons behind these moves, and challenge the government policies which are undermining inclusive and high-quality education.'

Report author Jo Hutchinson said: 'For the first time, we begin to see the full scale of this problem, having stripped away cases where family decisions have led to school moves.

'Our estimate is that one in 12 children are being pushed around the system, and that this has risen in recent years. We will undertake further research on these trends this year, highlighting prevalence among local areas and groups of schools.'

Geoff Barton, general secretary of the Association of School and College Leaders, said: 'The number of unexplained exits uncovered in the research is worryingly high, and the fact that certain vulnerable pupil groups are particularly likely to be affected is also worrying. However, we should keep in mind that many parents make the decision to move or home-school their child for their own reasons and without any pressure being applied.'

Anntoinette Bramble, chair of the Local Government Association's Children and Young People Board, said: 'Councils have serious concerns about the extent of off-rolling and other abuses in the system, which is why they need to be given new powers and funding so they can monitor and take action where necessary.'

The Department for Education said: 'No headteacher goes into the job to remove a pupil from school – and no headteacher takes the decision to do so lightly. Schools will typically have gone through a number of sanctions before exclusion is considered, taking into account the welfare of other pupils in the classroom.

'It is against the law to remove pupils on the basis of academic results – any school that does it is breaking the law. We have written to all schools to remind them of the rules on exclusions, and Edward Timpson is currently reviewing how schools use them and why some groups of children are more likely to be excluded from school than others.'

18 April 2019

Everyone welcome: inside the schools that haven't expelled a child since 2013

As the Government tries to curb high exclusion rates in England, one academy trust is proudly 'on-rolling' – open to all.

By Jess Staufenberg

Jason Thurley, headteacher at Beacon academy, near Grimsby, leans across the table explaining why yet another of his pupils was excluded before joining the school. 'He'd brought in a £1 potato gun. It was at the bottom of his bag and so he goes up to his form tutor and says, "I don't want to get into trouble with this, sir, can you take it?" And he gets permanently excluded. The school said "we have a zero-tolerance policy on firearms".'

Thurley laughs in disbelief. The same boy is now a year 10 sports leader who helps organise cross-country championships. He's just one of dozens of pupils who joined the school after being booted out of another one.

Of the current year 11s, 51% began their secondary education elsewhere. In year 10, it's 58%. Where are they all coming from?

Almost one-fifth of the year 10s were 'managed moves', meaning their school excluded them or was about to and had asked other heads to take them in. The rest arrived from pupil referral units, moved into the area, or, like the head boy, had previously been home educated. One pupil arrived after trying to burn down an art block. Another was rejected by three schools before Beacon took him.

Taking as many vulnerable pupils as possible – and never excluding them – is core to Thurley's mission in this deprived coastal corner of north-east Lincolnshire. His stance reflects the values of the sponsor, the Wellspring academy trust.

Since the trust was formed in 2013 not one student has been permanently excluded at any of its 20 schools – although 10 of those schools are primaries, which tend to have low exclusion rates anyway. Beacon is the only secondary, with the capacity for 750 pupils, but just 342 on its roll. The trust also has six alternative provision and three special educational needs schools, and bills itself as promoting inclusion and compassionate leadership as its central philosophy.

The trust summarises this approach as 'positive regard', and last September rebranded one school as the Positive Regard Teaching School. The school trains staff, led by the Springwell special academy in Barnsley, and has delivered specialist behaviour support packages to 84 schools across 15 local authorities. The training focuses on development trauma and attachment difficulties.

For Thurley, it means never giving up on the pupil. 'You have your lines, but you persevere. So you say, look, sorry, you

can't fight, and you talk about it, and in some cases that might be a short fixed-term exclusion. Then they come back and you've moved on. And then there's another bump in the road. Then we move on. In the end we get there.' I ask if the same would apply if, say, a student was found with a knife? He considers, having taken in pupils excluded for the same. 'I would look to keep them in the school.'

It's a far cry from the strict behaviour policies and high exclusion rates of some academy chains, such as Outwood Grange academies trust and Delta academies trust, which have attracted controversy over exclusions. Thurley says these trusts are in a 'different bracket'.

Now the Government is cracking down on exclusions amid concerns about 'off-rolling' – removing students to boost results. Last week a survey published by Ofsted reported that one in four teachers had witnessed apparent off-rolling. And the Department for Education (DfE) announced that schools would be held accountable for the results of pupils they exclude, a recommendation from the long-awaited exclusions review by Edward Timpson, who warns that 'it cannot be right to have a system where some schools could stand to improve their performance and finances through exclusion'. The report reveals that eight out of 10 expelled pupils in England come from vulnerable backgrounds.

Beacon academy can provide hope in this effort to encourage heads to be more inclusive. Ofsted judged it good three months ago, despite a -0.22 progress score and only 4% of pupils entering the EBacc, against a local average of 33%.

One parent was so anxious about her child's behaviour during the inspection that she rang Thurley to ask, 'do you want me to keep him off?' – an offer he refused. The parent later said she'd sent Ofsted a 1,000-character review praising the school, and would have written more except for the word limit.

Parental endorsements such as this perhaps explain why many of Wellspring's academies have strong Ofsted grades. Of the 13 schools inspected, two are outstanding, seven are good, and only one requires improvement – although the report still praised the school's leadership. This may be food for thought for trusts that defend tough behaviour policies as the way to raise standards.

Inspectors seem to be listening, too. Mark Wilson, Wellspring trust's chief executive, says Beacon's lead inspector accepts Thurley's view that the academy is, in effect, 'on-rolling' pupils – in other words, the school is single-handedly ensuring pupils are on the roll somewhere good. 'There are a number of youngsters who wouldn't be in education were it not for Beacon academy,' he says.

Yet Beacon's highly inclusive approach is a hard road, as the school is judged by the criteria applying to mainstream

education – and has the same funding, receiving £4,600 per pupil. By contrast, Phoenix Park alternative provision academy, a specialist provider in Grimsby also run by the Wellspring trust, receives £18,000 per pupil.

Jo Indian, head of Key Stage 2–3 at Phoenix Park, and Dave Mills, its executive vice-principal, both left mainstream education because of the pressures. 'Mainstream teachers don't have the luxury of being able to focus on pupils' needs because of the accountability measures,' says Indian – alternative provider such as Phoenix aren't judged on progress scores or Ebacc entries.

Back at Beacon, Thurley says as a mainstream school, he will struggle to keep taking so many 'managed moves' from other schools. And he does not entirely welcome the DfE's pledge to make schools accountable for excluded pupils, fearing his staff's hard work might not be recognised. 'Where children have come here from other schools and done well, why give other schools the results?' he asks.

While there are clearly significant challenges ahead, for now, the Wellspring trust is dedicating itself to spreading the word. It is developing a master's degree in compassionate leadership with Leeds Beckett University, which will include exclusion ethics. Three more alternative provision schools are opening shortly and Wilson is planning secondaries too. Any new schools will 'replicate the inclusive ethos at Beacon', he promises.

So will stricter academy trusts be converted? Perhaps inspectors aren't the only ones watching.

14 May 2019

'Little robots': behind the scenes at an academy school

New research from the Faculty of Education lifts the lid on an influential academy school, and finds an authoritarian system that reproduces race and class inequalities.

Structure liberates: the ethos behind one of England's flagship academy schools.

Designed as an engine of social mobility, this school drills 'urban children' for the grades and behaviour considered a passport to the world of middle-class salaries and sensibilities.

The headline-grabbing exam results of this school have led politicians to champion its approach as a silver bullet for entrenched poverty, and 'structure liberates' has become the blueprint for recent urban education reform.

The school's recipe has now been replicated many times through academy trusts that have spread like 'modern-day missionaries' across the nation, says Dr Christy Kulz, a Leverhulme Research Fellow at Cambridge's Faculty of Education. Shortly after it opened, Kulz was granted permission to conduct fieldwork in the school, where she had once worked as a teaching assistant. Choosing to anonymise her research, she calls the school Dreamfields.

Her new book goes behind the scenes of life at Dreamfields, and is the only detailed ethnographic account of the everyday practices within this new breed of academy school. 'Education has long been promoted as a salve that cures urban deprivation and balances capitalism's inequalities,' says Kulz, who spent 18 months of observation in Dreamfields, interviewing parents, teachers and students.

'The academy programme taps into 'mythical qualities' of social mobility: some kind of magic formula that provides equal opportunities for every individual once they are within the school, regardless of race, class or social context.' In 2012, then Prime Minister David Cameron described academies as 'working miracles'.

Primarily state funded but run as not-for-profit businesses, sometimes with support from individual philanthropists, academies such as Dreamfields are independent of local authority control and sit outside the democratic process of local government.

'Verbal cane'

The gospel according to Dreamfields' celebrated head is described as a 'traditional approach'. Kulz says she found a stress-ridden hierarchical culture focused on a conveyer belt of testing under strict – almost military – conditions, and suffused with police-style language of 'investigations' and 'repeat offenders'.

Enforcement comes through what Kulz calls the 'verbal cane'. Tongue-lashings administered by teachers regularly echoed around the corridors, and were encouraged by senior staff. One teacher told Kulz that seeing tall male members of staff screaming in the faces of 11-year-olds was 'very hard to digest'.

This verbal aggression is heightened by the panoptic surveillance built into the very architecture of the school. All activity is conducted within the bounds of a U-shaped building with a complete glass frontage. Everyone is on show at all times, including staff, who felt constantly monitored and pressured into visibly exerting the discipline favoured by management.

Policing was not confined to within the school gates. Kulz goes on a ride-along with what's known as 'chicken-shop patrol'. Driving around the streets after school, staff members jump out of the car to intervene when children are deemed to be congregating or in scruffy uniforms.

Stopping off at one of the local takeaways is considered a major offence. 'Fried chicken represents a "poor choice" that Dreamfields must prohibit in order to change urban culture,' says Kulz. 'Simply being caught in a takeaway after school is punished with a two-hour detention the following day.'

Students are also policed through exacting uniform adherence, with a 'broken-window theory' approach that sees deviation as opening the door to chaos.

The smallest rule infraction can be met with a spell in isolated detention. Staff would sometimes go to strange lengths to maintain conformity, she says. Suede shoes were subject to clampdown. Parental suggestions of a karaoke stall at a winter fair were considered far too risky. 'There is no room for unpredictability at Dreamfields,' says Kulz. One student who shaved lines into his eyebrows had to have them coloured in by a teacher every morning.

'Cultural cloning'

As fieldwork progressed, Kulz began to notice discrepancies that tallied uncomfortably with race and social background. Black children with fringes, or children who congregated outside takeaways, were reprimanded immediately. White middle-class children with long floppy hair, or gathering en masse by Tesco, were ignored. Teachers troubled by this would hint at it in hushed tones.

'The approach of many academy schools is one of cultural cloning,' says Kulz. 'The Dreamfields creed is that "urban children", a phrase used by staff to mean working-class and ethnic minority kids assumed to have unhappy backgrounds, need salvaging – with middle-class students positioned as the unnamed, normative and universal ideal.'

'Black students were consistently more heavily policed in the playground, resulting in many consciously adopting "whiter" styles and behaviours – a tactic that reduced their surveillance.' It is not just children who are driven hard through incessant monitoring. Staff at Dreamfields are subject to 'teacher tracking', a rolling system in which student grades are converted into scores, allowing management to rank the teachers – an approach staff compared with salesmen being judged on their weekly turnover.

This pressurised auditing resulted in rote learning to avoid a red flag in the system. 'You put a grade in that satisfies the system instead of it satisfying the student's knowledge and needs,' one teacher confessed to Kulz, explaining his 'real job' was not to teach understanding of his subject, but to get students to produce a set product quickly and accurately. One student described himself to Kulz as a 'little robot'.

Most teachers exceeded a 48-hour week. The majority of staff were young – an average age of 33 – with fewer outside commitments, yet many expressed a sense of exhaustion. 'If you're not in a lesson, we are expected to patrol,' one teacher told Kulz. 'Every moment of every day is taken up with some sort of duty.' Unlike most schools, Dreamfields has no staff room.

Some staff discussed former colleagues who had suffered burnout or were asked to resign. During interviews, Kulz found conspiracy theories were rife among students because of the number of teachers that 'just disappeared'.

Yet Dreamfields was – and still is – fêted by politicians and the media for its undeniably extraordinary exam results: over 80% pass rate at GCSE in an area where this was previously unthinkable. At the time, the school was vastly oversubscribed, with over 1,500 applications for just 200 places.

'Most of the students, parents and teachers were keen to comply to Dreamfields' regime, despite its injustices. The school's approach was seen as the best shot at securing grades and succeeding in an increasingly precarious economy,' says Kulz. 'Students, like staff, are trained to be expendable while the ideals of democracy and critical thinking we are allegedly meant to cherish are quashed in the process.'

This model of a disciplinarian school built for surveillance and which teaches market-force obedience has marched ever onward since her time in Dreamfields, says Kulz – arriving at new poverty front-lines such as rundown seaside towns. Yet grassroots resistance to this style of education is increasing. Last year, a recently established academy in Great Yarmouth that forbade 'slouching and talking in corridors' had pupils pulled out by parents objecting to the 'draconian' rules that are central to the much-imitated Dreamfields playbook.

Kulz believes the grades achieved by these schools – far from universally high – come at a price. 'We cannot continue to ignore the links between the testing regimes we put pupils through, the harsh school cultures they create, and the deteriorating physical and mental health of children and young people in the UK.'

11 April 2018

Inequality of education in the UK among highest of rich nations

THE CONVERSATION

An article from **The Conversation.**

By Kate Pickett, Professor of Epidemiology, University of York

Many people, across the political spectrum, see education as the key to solving all inequalities. If children have equal opportunities and access to quality education, then all will be well. But, as a new report shows, rich countries vary widely in how big the gap is between the educational achievement of rich and poor children.

Unicef's report, *An Unfair Start*, looks at educational inequalities in 41 of the world's richest countries, covering inequalities from access to early childhood education to expectations of post-secondary education.

The UK ranks 16th from the top in terms of educational inequality during the secondary school years, which doesn't sound too terrible, but the UK come 23rd in inequalities during the primary school years. These are depressing scores for the world's fifth-largest economy.

Income inequality

But this is not the first time the UK has ranked badly in supporting children in comparison to other countries. And research has shown that child well-being is directly linked with income inequality. So because the UK hasn't done much to reduce high levels of income inequality over the past decade, there hasn't been much change in how well British children are doing.

In 2007, Unicef published its first report on child well-being in rich countries. The UK, shockingly, ranked at the very bottom – with worse child well-being than any other country. There was also shown to be a strong and significant link between a country's level of income inequality – the gap between rich and poor – and how well children were doing.

Since then, Unicef has repeated the exercise of comparing rich countries – with reports in 2013 and 2016. Across many dimensions of child well-being, the UK does badly, often outranked by much poorer countries, such as Portugal and Eastern European nations.

Low-quality education

Tackling educational inequalities does not have to mean sacrificing high standards. In fact, the new Unicef report shows that countries with higher average achievement have lower gaps in reading scores between the best and the worst readers. At primary school, the Netherlands does particularly well, with high average performance and a small gap. New Zealand does particularly badly, with a low average and a large gap in performance.

It is also clear that high income is no guarantee of high educational quality. Some of the poorer countries in the group – Latvia, Estonia, Croatia – do better than some of the wealthier counties, such as the UK, US or Sweden.

The report also shows that girls consistently do better than boys. And migrant children do less well than non-migrant children in most countries – although in Australia and Canada, second-generation immigrant children outperform non-migrant children.

Family backgrounds is also shown to be a key driver of attainment and inequalities. Children from lower social class backgrounds lag behind their peers from richer, higher social class backgrounds from preschool onwards. None of this is news, these facts are well known by educational researchers and teachers alike.

How to make it better

There's also the issue that affordability of preschool and childcare creates a barrier to access for many families. Research shows that in countries where there is more of a gap between rich and poor families who have children in early childhood education, fewer children overall attend. And in London, for example, even when there is some free preschool provision, children from more affluent areas are most likely to take up places. Educational inequalities are also worse when there is more segregation of rich and poor children in schools.

Unicef are cautious in their proposals to reduce educational inequalities. They call for better data and more attention to equality rather than average attainment, more attention to gender stereotypes and the gender mix of the teaching profession, and a focus on basic skills.

They also call for high-quality early education and care to be guaranteed for all children. But stop short of suggesting it should be free for all. In their boldest proposal they suggest that welfare and benefits for families and less socioeconomic segregation in schools will help to mitigate educational inequalities.

But we need to be more radical if we want to reduce educational inequalities: turn to solving the deep-seated root causes at their source. This can be done by creating economies where child well-being is a central and overarching aim – not something that's only thought about every few years, when Unicef reveals how future generations are being failed.

30 October 2018

Hundreds of councillors urge government to pump billions of pounds into cash-strapped schools

'The cuts to school budgets have reached epidemic levels,' letter to Damian Hinds warns.

By Eleanor Busby

Hundreds of local councillors are calling on the Education Secretary to urge the Government to pump billions of pounds into funding schools.

In a letter to Damian Hinds, signed by more than 1,000 councillors, they say many schools are now 'desperately overwhelmed' as more students are competing for fewer resources.

The current situation is 'not tenable' amid cuts to local council services and a recruitment and retention crisis across the profession, they add.

It follows a report by the Institute for Fiscal Studies (IFS) last year which said total school spending per pupil in England has fallen by 8% in real terms between 2009–10 and 2017–18.

Headteachers across the country have spoken out about squeezed budgets forcing them to have to ask parents for basic essentials like toilet roll, while some have had to shorten the school week.

The letter, due to be handed in to the Department for Education (DfE) in Westminster, says: 'Many schools are now desperately overwhelmed as more and more students are competing for fewer and fewer resources. Compounded by biting cuts to local council services, in addition to the teacher recruitment and retention crisis, the current settlement is not tenable.'

Southwark councillor Maggie Browning, the National Education Union's (NEU) councillors network convener, said: 'The cuts to school budgets have reached epidemic levels in England and Wales. Increasingly, tighter funds mean schools across the country are narrowing their curriculum and cutting subjects like drama and art, which is a travesty.'

She added: 'Teachers' workloads have become unsustainable as they are asked to do more and more with less, including larger class sizes and fuller timetables with less support.'

Ms Browning said that this was 'fuelling' the recruitment and retention crisis across the country, adding it was 'deeply disruptive' to the learning of students.

The letter comes as a new study from the UCL Institute of Education has found that nearly half of new teachers consider leaving within 10 years.

More than two in three said their main reason for wanting to teach was to 'make a difference' – however, once they started teaching, the reality of daily life as a teacher dulled their enthusiasm.

For those who had left, the reasons given were to improve work/life balance (75%), workload (71%), and a target-driven culture (57%).

A DfE spokesman said: 'School funding in England is at its highest ever level and since 2017 the Government has given every local authority in England more money for every pupil in every school, while allocating the biggest increases to the schools that have been most underfunded.

'In the last year we have also announced an extra £400 million of capital funding for schools from the Treasury. Nonetheless, we do recognise the budgeting challenges schools face. That is why the Education Secretary has been making a strong case for education spending across government ahead of the next spending review.'

2 April 2019

Two-thirds of school heads have cut teachers to save money

Over two-thirds (69%) of secondary school heads have had to cut teaching staff to save money, according to new polling published by the Sutton Trust today.

The survey of 1,678 teachers, conducted by the National Foundation for Educational Research (NFER) for the Trust as part of their Teacher Voice Omnibus Survey, highlights how budget cuts are affecting schools across the country.

While a much smaller proportion (32%) of senior leaders in primary schools said they'd had to cut teachers, almost two-thirds of this group (72%) reported cutting teaching assistants. Two-fifths (41%) of primary and secondary school heads said they'd had to cut back on trips and outings, while over a half (55%) said they'd slashed spending on IT equipment.

Analysis by the Institute for Fiscal Studies found that the amount of per-pupil spending in England's schools fell by 8% in real terms between 2009–10 and 2017–18.

The teachers were also asked about how they spend their pupil premium, which is additional money paid for every disadvantaged pupil in a school and intended to close the attainment gap. One–quarter (27%) of secondary school heads said they used it to plug gaps elsewhere in their budget, most of this group said it was used to pay for teachers and teaching assistants instead. Heads in the most deprived schools were twice as likely to report using their pupil premium money to plug budget gaps as those in the least deprived schools (34% v 17%).

A majority (55%) of school leaders said that their pupil premium funding is helping to close attainment gaps in their school, with primary leaders more likely (58%) than secondary heads (50%) to say so. Of those who don't think the pupil premium is having an impact, many said the funding is not enough to make an impact, or is being spent in other areas. Heads who reported having to plug budget gaps were less likely to say that attainment gaps were closing (62% v 40%). Many also pointed out the difficulty in closing their attainment gaps given factors outside the school gates.

When it comes to deciding which programmes and approaches to adopt to improve learning, the use of evidence continues to rise. Three-quarters (74%) of all senior leaders said they considered research evidence, with 70% of secondary school senior leaders citing the Education Endowment Foundation's Teaching and Learning Toolkit. This is up 7 percentage points from 63% last year to 70% this year. Secondary teachers who reported using research evidence were more likely to report that their pupil premium money was proving effective (46% v 32%).

The Sutton Trust is urging the Government to address the funding issues and financial uncertainty that schools are facing. They would like the promised spending review to take place as soon as possible to provide funding clarity for schools, as well as continued support for disadvantaged pupils paid through the pupil premium.

Sir Peter Lampl, founder and executive chairman of the Sutton Trust and chairman of the Education Endowment Foundation, said:

'Our new polling adds to the growing evidence that the squeeze on school budgets is having a detrimental effect. Of particular concern is that schools are having to use funding for poorer pupils to plug gaps in their finances. Many are having to get rid of teachers to close these funding gaps and endangering efforts to improve opportunities for poorer young people.

'It is good to see more and more schools using evidence – and particularly the Teaching and Learning Toolkit – to decide how to spend their pupil premium. Using evidence of what has worked in the past is the best way to judge what is likely to work in the future. So it is no surprise that those teachers who said they use research evidence were more likely to think their pupil premium money was proving effective.'

18 April 2019

Make a wish: the schools forced to use Amazon to ask parents to buy pens

Schools are asking for toys, books, and 'scientific slime' via Amazon wishlists as unions warn budgets have reached a breaking point.

By Pippa Allen-Kinross

Schools Week conducted a search of schools' publicly-available wishlists across England and found hundreds have shopping lists using which parents and alumni can help stock libraries and provide stationery.

Donors have paid for objects as varied as a box of essential oils (£42.95), a three-in-one tent, tunnel and ballpit (£25.95) and a multipack of post-it notes (£27.29).

Leading unions say this is the latest sign of the 'severe funding pressures facing schools', but the Department for Education insists that schools have enough money for resources.

Among the thousands of lists with 'school' in their names hosted by the online shopping giant, four of the most recent belong to Ark, an academy trust with over 30 schools across England.

Ark said that two lists were established by the library or friends of the school to allow parents to donate books for the school library but both are now redundant. It denied the two other lists were connected to its schools'.

'Ark Schools do not use Amazon wishlists to promote purchasing items for pupils by parents or guardians, however if local parents' associations and or individual parents wish to support their local Ark school in this way we of course welcome their generosity,' a spokesperson said.

The Wroxham School, a primary in Hertfordshire, has a list which asks for people to lend their 'generosity' in buying a new book for the school which could 'help transport a child to a new land or open endless possibilities'.

The list opened last year and 13 books have already been purchased, for a total of £70. Wroxham did not respond to requests for comment.

Gibside School, a special primary school in Newcastle, says on its wishlist that it is 'always looking for additional resources which will help our children achieve their full potential. Any funding or support will make a huge difference to our school'.

It wants slime for 'scientific exploration' (£1.12) and a dolls head mannequin for £18.99 to help autistic children prepare for trips to the hairdresser by modelling the combing and washing of hair.

Sussex-based Halsford Park Primary School's list says it was created by the teachers, and that 'this wishlist is for parents and relatives to buy something the school needs. No one can do everything, but everyone can do something.'

It includes 30 sets of handwriting pens at £2.49 each, 20 multipacks of Pritt Stick (£30.47 each) and a £4.99 rubber ball for the playground.

The wishlists are not just used by primary schools. Newstead Wood School, a girls' grammar school in outer London, asks for help in stocking its library, saying: 'Please help support your library and future generations of Newstead Wood students by donating a book.'

Over 200 books have been purchased, with the most recent including a book about Shakespeare for £15.99 and a Pelican introductory book on Russia for £6.99.

Hertfordshire & Essex High School also uses a wish list, but a spokesperson said the girls' school's list was a 'positive' way to allow its alumni network to donate books and 'give back to the school in some way' rather than a consequence of budget cuts.

A survey of 238 school business leaders by the Association of School and College Leaders released earlier this month revealed 20 per cent had asked parents for voluntary contributions over the last year, and 24 per cent expected to have to do so in the next 12 months.

However, a spokesperson for the Department for Education insisted that 'we provide schools with funding to buy the resources they need'.

'If schools are requesting voluntary contributions, they must always make clear to parents that these are voluntary only and they are under no obligation to contribute in any way,' they added.

Geoff Barton, ASCL's general secretary, said school budgets have been cut by £2.8 billion since 2015 and wishlists are 'another sign of the severe funding pressures facing schools'.

Paul Whiteman, the general secretary of the National Association of Head Teachers, said the entire state-funded school system 'is rapidly heading towards insolvency' and schools must receive more funding in the autumn budget 'if not before'.

'Two or three years ago, no school would have been considering Amazon wishlists, but the real-terms cuts to school budgets since 2015 are having a big impact on the quality of education now,' he said.

25 May 2018

Are school uniforms a violation of freedom of expression?

By Noshin Jannat

Freedom of expression is a fundamental human right we have been given which cannot be taken away from us. As a democratic society, everyone is entitled to this right. However, in the case of school uniforms, we must recognise this is not a breach of the liberty to expression, but it simply goes against some children's clothing preferences. Therefore, this essay will argue why school uniform does not violate our right to expression, by exploring the purpose of school uniform and the idea that uniforms do not forbid us from wearing other items we also have the right to wear, like the hijab.

Firstly, it is important to consider the benefits and purpose of school uniform, which is to ensure everyone is grouped together consistently as a school. There are benefits to this, such as children do not have to worry about clothes, or outfits. Some argue that focus on appearance takes away focus on schoolwork, which is why children should not have to be preoccupied with how they dress to school. Also, it is simply more practical. For example, when classes go on school trips, it is easier to identify schools and keep track of them if they are wearing their school's uniform. Overall, school uniforms ensure consistency and have many advantages, like allowing children to not get too caught up with how they dress and increasing safety when going on trips by being able to easily track where the students are.

On the other hand, one could argue that school uniforms are a violation to our freedom of expression. This is because by enforcing uniforms, we are not allowing children to express themselves how they please by wearing the colours or patterns that they want to wear. Arguably, for some children, being able to choose their own outfits provides a creative means to express themselves and their personality. However, it is also argued that this is not a breach of our right to expression – it merely goes against children's preferences which is not equivalent. This is because school uniforms remove our choice, which goes against people's individual preferences for colours, designs and more, but it does not remove our right to also wear items that represent identity, like the ability to wear a hijab in school. For many, religion is their identity, and uniform does not remove or 'water down' our identity. Contrastingly, in France, religious items like the hijab and symbols of a cross are not allowed anywhere, as they have not been since 2004. This, arguably, violates freedom of expression and freedom of conscience, thought and religion, but UK rules on uniform do not. Therefore, it is important to distinguish between preference and liberty to expression and understand that in the UK, uniforms do not forbid us from wearing items that represent personal identities, like the hijab, even though rules in France do ban these symbols.

Next, one must understand how uniforms do not violate our freedom of expression. For example, many schools require students to use specific pens – which are generally black and non-ink – to use during exams. Another example is that when working, employees are generally not allowed to wear rings – particularly in food places – to ensure hygiene. Neither examples show breaches to our rights to expression, they simply show that sometimes certain pens or rings are not appropriate in certain cases for many reasons – just as wearing clothes that are not in the uniform is inappropriate because it removes consistency and is more impractical (due to reasons discussed earlier). Thus, sometimes it is inappropriate to wear certain items to school.

Overall, school uniforms are not a breach of our freedom of expression because children are allowed to express their identity by wearing items like the hijab and crosses in the UK. They merely go against personal preferences for colour and design. There are many more benefits to having a uniform than disadvantages; for example, they ensure safety on school trips. However, perhaps some schools should start allowing students to have more of a vote in what the uniform looks like to ensure everyone feels comfortable and confident. Also, it seems more important to focus on the issues of banning make-up in school, which goes against freedom of expression by removing what makes people feel more comfortable in their own skin and maintaining a healthy self-esteem.

12 December 2018

www.theylj.co.uk

School uniform costs force families into debt

One million children live in families across England who are getting into debt to meet the rising cost of school uniforms – a new study by The Children's Society has found.

This is based on responses to a new survey by The Children's Society, which found that 13% of parents were getting into debt to cover costs of school uniform – up from 7% when the charity conducted the same survey in 2015.

According to responses from 1,000 parents, nearly one in six families said school uniform costs were to blame for them having to cut back on food and other basic essentials compared to one in seven in 2015.

The report, *The Wrong Blazer 2018*: *Time for action on school uniform costs*, an update of The Children's Society's survey from 2015, reveals families are shelling out more on school uniforms with an average of £340 per year for each child at secondary school – an increase of 7% or £24 since 2015. Parents of primary school children spent on average £255, an increase of 2% since 2015.

The Government pledged three years ago to clamp down on school uniform costs, to make it a legal requirement for schools to put value for money as the top consideration when sourcing school uniforms, but has yet to do so.

The high cost of uniforms can be put down in part to school policies that make parents buy clothing from specialist shops rather than giving them the choice of buying items at cheaper stores such as supermarkets or high-street chains. Where parents have to buy two or more items of school uniform from a specific supplier, spending was found to be an average of £71 per year higher for secondary school children and £77 higher for primary school children.

For children themselves, the cost of school uniform can have a serious impact. Around one in 10 parents said it had led to their child wearing uniform that didn't fit properly, and more than one in 20 said that their child had been sent home for wearing the wrong clothes or shoes as a result of them struggling to afford the cost.

Based on these results and Department for Education statistics on numbers of children in primary and secondary schools across England, it's estimated that around 1.7 million children go to school wearing incorrect, unclean or ill-fitting uniform and half a million children have been sent home because of wearing the wrong items.

The report finds that parents of secondary age children pay the most for different items of clothing with coats and bags the most expensive items, both costing £57 annually for each child. They are followed by school shoes averaging at £48 each per year and blazers at £39. PE kits and trousers, skirts and dresses are also expensive with an average price tag of £41 for secondary school pupils.

These figures are staggering when compared to the amount parents feel is reasonable to spend on uniforms in total in a year. Parents of both primary and secondary school children felt on average that they were paying around three times too much. The survey found parents of children at primaries pay £174 more than the £81 that they feel would be reasonable to pay and parents of children and secondary schools pay £225 more than the £115 that they feel would be reasonable.

The research finds school uniform costs are having a greater impact on more families than in 2015. Whilst much of this may be due to rising costs, The Children's Society says another major reason is likely to be the squeeze on family incomes caused by reduced financial support – including the current four-year freeze on key benefits and tax credits.

The Children's Society is calling for action from government to act on the pledge they made in 2015 to make guidance on school uniform legally binding, so that cost is always a key priority in setting school uniform policy.

Matthew Reed, Chief Executive at The Children's Society said: 'It's truly shocking that so many families are affected by the excessive and unaffordable price tag on school uniforms, forcing thousands to cut back on food and heating or having to borrow money to cover the costs. It's also damaging children's wellbeing and in many cases, getting in the way of their education.

'Too many parents still face having to buy a number of items from specialist suppliers, when they could pick up similar items at cheaper stores and supermarkets. We want the Government to fulfil the commitment it made in 2015 and enforce legally binding rules which ensure that schools make the cost to families a top priority in setting school uniform policy. This change would potentially save families hundreds of millions of pounds, without costing the Government a penny.

23 August 2018

Primary school homework – just how much should children be getting?

Comedian Rob Delaney fired up a debate on homework this week – here's a look back on what people had to say about it.

By Florence Snead

For many parents, getting their children to do homework can be a daily battle – but is it even that important?

The debate over how much work youngsters should be doing outside the classroom fired up again this week following a tweet from the US comedian and actor Rob Delaney.

Delaney, who stars in Channel 4 sitcom *Catastrophe*, garnered dozens of responses after he addressed the subject to his one-and-half million followers.

'Who knows more about stopping this madness?'

'Why do they give 7 yr olds so much homework in UK & how do I stop this,' he wrote. 'I want my kid frolicking and drawing and playing football. Who knows more about stopping this madness and can help me?'

He continued: 'Love our kids' school and teachers (including heads) just sense they're being told to "teach to the test" just like in America, where people are obviously stupid.'

It wasn't long before hundreds of replies flooded in, with everyone from teachers and parents to household names weighing in to have their say.

The comedian Romesh Ranganathan – a former maths teacher – would scrap homework altogether. 'It's absolutely ridiculous,' he replied.

'There should be none. The idea that homework at that age is the best use of their time is so insane. It causes stress, ruins evenings and for no real furthering of learning. Can you tell I'm against?'

Football pundit Gary Lineker agreed. 'Homework is a waste of time,' wrote the *Match of the Day* presenter.

'Brings stress to the home, stress to the child, stress to the parents, stress to the parent-child relationship. Reading every night should suffice.'

The former England star said lots of parents appeared to agree "on the pointlessness and stressful nature" of homework'.

He argued children should be allowed to play and enjoy their home life without having to do extra work.

'There's plenty of time to be an adult', he added.

As for Jason Manford, he thought Delaney was 'bang on'. The comedian said there was no need for primary school children to have homework other than reading a book they wanted.

'In a time where mental health is critical, it's important for kids and adults to realise that their free time is theirs to do with what they like,' he said.

Some parents 'ask for more'

But not everyone hates homework and some parents even ask for more, Delaney was told.

Twitter user Bernadette Stott said homework in primary school was 'nuts' but there were 'parents who don't think they get enough and ask for more'.

And teacher Flora Marge replied: 'Most parents actually complain when you don't set homework. We can't win.'

Others could see the positives. One suggested that homework helped to ease children into independent study as they moved towards secondary school.

'But at that age it should only be reading or spellings, basic maths and maybe something creative,' they added.

But perhaps the fiercest riposte came from *Good Morning Britain* presenter Piers Morgan. 'A lot of LAZY parents will agree with you, Jugs,' he wrote. 'As a nation, we're falling so far behind educational standards of countries like China, it's embarrassing.

'Telling our kids now to give up on homework seems a perverse response to this.'

It is far from the first time that homework has hit the headlines. A national furore erupted in 2016 when a school in Essex – albeit a secondary – announced it was scrapping it.

Catherine Hutley, then principal of the Philip Morant School and College in Colchester, admitted at the time it was a controversial move but said marking placed a huge burden on teachers.

Earlier this year it was reported that the policy had been abandoned.

Previous guidelines 'too bureaucratic'

Schools have been free to make up their own minds about homework since 2012, after former Education Secretary Michael Gove did away with previous guidelines set by Labour in 1997.

The Labour Government had recommended an hour a week for five- to seven-year-olds, rising to half an hour a night for seven- to 11-year-olds and two and a half hours a night for pupils aged between 14 and 16.

But Gove said the advice was 'too bureaucratic'. His decision followed complaints from some parents that too much homework limited family time and opportunities for play and sport.

Louise Regan, who has been a primary school head in Nottingham for 18 years, told *i* she was not opposed to homework – but that it needs to be appropriate for the child.

Primary school children, she said, could be pretty tired at the end of the day and homework could also be a 'big ask' for parents who might be working multiple jobs or lack the resources and space at home.

Then there are the teachers to consider. Setting homework can add to their already vast workloads, she said.

'Children learn in lots of ways so doing something at home with your parents or going shopping is a good learning experience. There are ways to learn separately from sitting down and doing formal work.

'Some children do dance after school, or swimming or taekwondo – those are all good things to do, we shouldn't stop those sorts of things happening.

'It's good if parents can read with kids and children get lots of exposure to books and can practise their spellings or times tables, they are really helpful.

'But equally we want kids to be happy to go outside and play, to go to the park and do those things. Any policy that a school has, has to have that flexibility.'

Evidence 'inconclusive'

Ms Regan considers the evidence 'inconclusive' as to whether or not homework benefits primary school children.

'I think the evidence is it's not one of the high-impact things in terms of a child's development,' she added.

Earlier this year a report from Ofsted revealed more than a third of parents (36 per cent) did not think homework was helpful 'at all' for their children at primary school.

The authority's 'Parent Panel' report revealed that while the majority of parents thought homework was useful, this was more the case for secondary pupils (87 per cent) than primary (64 per cent).

Nearly three-quarters of parents (72 per cent) said they thought prep at school – allowing pupils time to plan and get ready for lessons through research – was a better alternative.

The report stated some parents spoke 'positively' about homework, saying it helped them to feel part of their child's learning and helped them improve their planning and time management skills.

'For some though, homework was a problem,' it continued. 'Many parents said homework was a huge cause of stress for the whole family and had a negative impact on home life.'

For the moment, it seems the jury is out.

28 September 2018

Is homework necessary or a pointless waste of time?

By Tijen Butler

There's an ongoing debate surrounding the necessity of homework for school children and young teenagers alike.

On one hand, homework can cause stress and the task may not have much substance to it, with most teachers merely setting it because they've been instructed to do so daily. But on the other flip of the coin, homework is necessary because the child can then gain a deeper understanding of a topic and they will grow up disciplined.

Which countries set the most homework?

The countries that prioritise homework are not actually the countries that do the best academically. This is a huge indicator that the home activity may be pointless.

The country that sets the most homework won't surprise you. China's primary and secondary school students spend around 3 hours a day doing homework. **This is twice the global average.**

This is followed by:

Russia, Singapore, Kazakhstan and then a European country which may surprise you…

According to OECD research, teenagers in Italy must commit up to nine hours per week. This makes Italy the number one EU country to set the most homework.

Other European countries such as Ireland, with teenagers spending over 7 hours of homework per week, Spain, and Hungary closely follow.

The United States sets around an hour more per week than the United Kingdom. However, they are both in the middle of the spectrum.

The country that sets the least homework is Finland, with only 2 hours per week. This is interesting because it is also said that **Finland has the best schooling system in the world.**

So, does that mean there's a link between less homework and academic success?

Or is it simply a coincidence and homework should be a continued practice?

What are the benefits of homework?

Of course, there are obvious pros and that's why the majority of schooling systems set several hours' worth of homework every week.

The after-school workload is an opportunity for families to get involved in the child's learning process, and it reinforces what has been taught that day at school, so the child can better understand and remember.

It can give parents an insight into what their child is struggling and exceeding in. Then, the parent could arrange private tuition in that area, if it was needed.

It also gives students various skills and life-lessons such as discipline, accountability, independence, time management and team-work. These will all be beneficial beyond school and it gives them a taste of 'real life'.

But then why can homework be a pointless waste of time?

Firstly, homework is handed out too frequently, making it stressful and boring.

Often, it's also too difficult for the child, even with the parent's help, increasing pressure and anxiety.

As a result of this, parents often do their child's homework instead. A survey shows that a hefty 23% of parents actually complete their child's homework assignments without even involving them.

What good would this do?

Another reason it could be a waste of time is the way in which teachers set it. They seem to set frivolous tasks for the sake of it. Unless the homework holds purpose, why bother doing it?

It may be better to set fewer hours on assignments that are truly meaningful, instead of 5+ hours on repetitive tasks – though not all schools would do this.

However, subjects such as maths will often always be beneficial because they work at practising equations… but, again, this only works if the child understands what they're doing.

What do the professionals think about this debate?

It seems that professionals in the education industry have taken opposing viewpoints. Let's find out who thinks what.

Some professionals say homework is 'completely pointless'

The director of the ResearchEd conference, Tom Bennett called homework 'completely pointless' when referring to the Ofsted regime which encourages teachers to set out more homework assignments for their students.

He believes that the after-school educational practice is 'back breaking' and he claimed that it actually steals away their family time.

Further validating this point, author Nicholson Baker said, 'No mandatory homework in elementary school. None. No homework in middle school and high school unless a kid wants to do it.'

He continued, 'Chronic nightly homework makes for guilt, resentment, and lies – and family arguments and bone weariness. Parents become enforcers. It gets ugly.'

Other professionals think that homework is 100% 'necessary'

Ms Ahrens, the director of education policy in Southeast Asia Resource Action Center believes in the importance of homework. She said, 'Homework is absolutely necessary for students to demonstrate that they are able to independently process and apply their learning.'

However, she does believe it can be changed in terms of the method so it's more beneficial. 'Homework might include pre-reading in preparation for what will be covered in class that day, independent research on a student-chosen topic that complements the class curriculum, experiential learning through a volunteer activity or field trip, or visiting a website and accomplishing a task on it.'

While some experts had a firm standpoint on the matter, some professionals were on the fence about the debate

It's likely that the majority of professionals sees both sides.

Richard Kahlenberg of The Century Foundation said, 'Homework, in the popular parlance, is thought of as a necessary but dreary component of education. But if properly envisioned, homework can be exhilarating, an opportunity for students to venture independently to pursue in-depth topics first broached in the classroom.'

In order to, therefore, make homework a positive thing, students must be excited by it and this can be done through a 'hands-on' approach. If you do this, there is a definite 'point' to homework.

Kahlenberg said, 'It will encourage students to be explorers and to move beyond what is familiar to them. It will take them into new neighbourhoods to interact with people of racial, ethnic and economic backgrounds different than their own.'

What does a GCSE Chief Examiner think?

Similarly, GCSE Chief Examiner Mark Richards can identify the benefits from setting homework, but he too sees the drawbacks in the way that homework is set. He wrote to me with his thoughts on whether homework was pointless.

Mark Richards said, 'Homework is not pointless per se. Having said that, it is all too easy for it to become largely ineffective. Furthermore, a poorly thought-through school homework policy can render it pointless.'

The GCSE examiner continued, 'Work that challenges, extends and builds on pupils' learning cannot ever really be pointless. But the problem is this: how often – genuinely – can the tasks that are typically set as homework be described as such?'

'In all honesty, setting Year 7 "something to do" on Tuesday because that is what it says should happen on the homework table is a recipe for disaster. Homework should only be set if it truly moves learning forward.'

And what do I think?

As someone who has researched this subject for the purposes of this article, as well as studied in school and university with a lot of homework assignments, it's clear to say I also have my own opinion on homework. It's very similar to Mark Richards', though perhaps leaning towards it being more pointless for the younger children.

I've always thought that the last thing a child needs is stress so constant homework should be avoided. However, a degree of discipline is definitely necessary, especially with

subjects the child struggles in because the time at school may not be enough.

Around 5 years old, I think homework is important for a child to gain the essential and core skills in each subject. It's also a way for them to learn with their parents and bond.

However, around the age of 10, I don't see the necessity. From my memory of education, homework at that age was also pointless. It did not provide me with any further substance for the topic. Indeed, they seemed to be mindless tasks, repeating what was already done in the classroom and not helping me any further.

Indeed, once kids grow up to GCSE level, it may become prudent to understand difficult subjects and pass exams. That's when homework may be necessary in order to cement things in the brain – because much of the testing system seems to be a memory test (and that's a separate issue entirely).

So... is it necessary?

While British children may not be happy with doing homework (because what child really likes it?), they should appreciate the fact that UK pupils only receive around 5 hours per week, compared to Shanghai, China's 14 hours.

However, are those 5 hours necessary? Why does Finland do so well when their students barely have any?

Well, homework does have clear benefits. With the skills mentioned above, as well as giving the parent's an insight into their child's performance, it looks like homework is here to stay.

Then again, there are definitely many homework tasks that may make your eyes roll as you question 'Why?'. The next time you see this kind of pointless homework set, whether you're the pupil or parent, why not question the teacher? Ask them what purpose it has and you may see the benefits.

12 March 2018

Key facts

- Academies were introduced through the Learning and Skills Act 2000 to boost struggling schools in deprived inner-city areas. (page 5)

- In 2017, research by the Education Policy Institute found turning schools into academies doesn't automatically improve standards, with the lowest performing primary and secondary schools in academy groups. (page 6)

- The 12% of countries where children start school at age 4 or 5 were all once part of the British Empire. (page 7)

- In studies by the UN, children in the UK rate very low on the tables for happiness. (page 8)

- Children who are younger than their peers when they start school are more likely to develop poorer mental health. (page 9)

- All children benefit from early schooling; however, the average effects are stronger for disadvantaged boys. (page 10)

- An additional term of early schooling boosted age five test scores in language and numeracy by 6-10% and age-seven language and numeracy skills by about two per cent. (page 10)

- In the 2016/2017 exam period Childline delivered over 3,000 counselling sessions about exam stress – this is a 2% increase from the previous year and an 11% increase from just two years prior. (page 15)

- Almost 40 per cent of Young Minds counselling sessions were related to exam stress. (page 15)

- Suicide rates among young people have also seen exponential rises of 67% since 2010. (page 16)

- A pick up in overall achievement of grade A/7 and above, or C/4 and above is driven by boys in particular. They've shown a slight increase in achievement of these grades, while achievement among girls is much the same as in previous years. (page 16)

- Both boys and girls saw dips in the proportion achieving grade A/7 or above from 2015 to 2017. (page 17)

- After a drop of around three percentage points from 2015 to 2017, boys' performance picked up by around one percentage point this year. (page 17)

- Overall, Northern Ireland continues to significantly outperform England and Wales. (page 17)

- The drop in performance in Wales is most notable – the 1.2 percentage point fall this year follows a 3.8 percentage point fall the year before. (page 17)

- Last year an outrageous 34% of university place offers were unconditional. (page 18)

- Around 15% of GCSE students may fall into the category of being 'highly test anxious'. (page 20)

- 73% of pupils who have over 95% attendance achieve five or more GCSEs at grades A*–C. (page 22)

- Morning classes have a high rate of absenteeism – especially 9.00am classes. (page 23)

- Female students miss fewer classes than male students. (page 23)

- Missing classes has an adverse effect, but only for 'high ability' students, and missing 10% of classes was associated with a 1-2 percentage point lower mark for this group of students. (page 23)

- Students who have performed well in their first year tend to have lower absenteeism rates in their second year. (page 23)

- 60,000 children, many of whom are vulnerable or have special educational needs, are permanently out of school and therefore effectively 'off the grid'. (page 24)

- The number of children who are known by councils to be home educated was 27% higher in 2018 than in 2017, and has risen by 20% in each of the last five years – doubling since 2013–14. (page 24)

- More than 49,000 pupils from a single cohort disappeared from the school rolls without explanation. (page 25)

- Just 330 schools, which constitute 6% of secondary schools in England, accounted for almost a quarter (23%) of the total number of unexplained moves in 2017. (page 25)

- The UK ranks 16th from the top in terms of educational inequality during the secondary school years. (page 30)

- In 2007, Unicef published its first report on child well-being in rich countries. The UK, shockingly, ranked at the very bottom. (page 30)

- A report by the Institute for Fiscal Studies (IFS) last year said total school spending per pupil in England has fallen by 8% in real terms between 2009–10 and 2017–18. (page 31)

- Nearly half of new teachers consider leaving within 10 years. (page 31)

- Over two-thirds (69%) of secondary school heads have had to cut teaching staff to save money. (page 32)

- 32% of senior leaders in primary schools said they'd had to cut teachers, almost two-thirds of this group (72%) reported cutting teaching assistants. (page 32)

- Two-fifths (41%) of primary and secondary school heads said they'd had to cut back on trips and outings, while over a half (55%) said they'd slashed spending on IT equipment. (page 32)

- 13% of parents were getting into debt to cover costs of school uniform. (page 35)

- School uniforms cost an average of £340 per year for each child at secondary school. (page 35)

- More than one in 20 parents said that their child had been sent home for wearing the wrong clothes or shoes as a result of them struggling to afford the cost. (page 35)

- Ofsted revealed more than a third of parents (36 per cent) did not think homework was helpful 'at all' for their children at primary school. (page 37)

- China's primary and secondary school students spend around 3 hours a day doing homework. (page 38)

- Irish teenagers spend over 7 hours of doing homework per week. (page 38)

- The country that sets the least homework is Finland, with only 2 hours per week. (page 38)

Academy

Academies (under the Academies Bill 2010) are schools that are state-maintained, but independently run and funded by external sponsors. This gives the school greater freedom from local authority bureaucracy; for example, how much they pay their staff and the subjects students are taught. Often, failing state schools are encouraged to apply for academy status.

A-levels

These are qualifications usually taken by students aged 16 to 18 at schools and sixth-form colleges, although they can be taken at any time by school leavers at local colleges or through distance learning. They provide an accepted route to degree courses and university and usually take two years to complete.

Comprehensive school

Also known as state schools, comprehensive schools are the state-run, government-funded schools in Britain. Education is free in comprehensive schools.

Faith school

A faith school is subject to the national curriculum, but is affiliated to a particular religious faith or denomination.

Free school

Free schools have the same freedoms and flexibilities as academies, but they do not normally replace an existing school. Free schools may be set up by a wide range of proposers – including charities, universities, businesses, educational groups, teachers and groups of parents.

Further education

Education for 16- to 18-year-olds, for example college or sixth form.

GCSE

This stands for General Certificate of Secondary Education; it is the national exam taken by 16-year-olds in England and Wales. The Scottish equivalent is the Scottish Certificate of Education.

Grammar school

Grammar schools are state secondary schools in England that select their pupils by ability. The examination taken to enter a grammar school is known as the 11-plus. Grammar schools in Wales and Scotland are non-selective.

IGCSE

Introduced in 1988, International GCSE is an alternative to the traditional GCSEs, offered by Cambridge and Edexcel exam boards.

International Baccalaureate (IB or IBac)

An alternative to A-levels, the IBac was developed in Switzerland and is highly regarded by universities.

National Curriculum

The statutory set of guidelines set down by the Government which determine the subject material and attainment targets taught in schools in England and Wales. The National Curriculum applies to pupils up to the age of 16.

SATs

End of Key Stage Tests and Assessments (more commonly known as SATs) are national tests that children take twice during their primary school life. First, at the end of Key Stage 1 (KS1) in Year 2, and then second at the end of Key Stage 2 (KS2) in Year 6.

Sixth form

Sixth form is a type of post-16 education which enables students to study for their A-levels or equivalents. Some sixth-form institutions are independent colleges, whilst others are attached to secondary schools.

State school

A school which is funded and run by the Government, at no cost to the pupils. An independent school, on the other hand, is one which is privately run and which pupils pay a fee to attend. These are sometimes known as 'private schools' or 'public schools' (please note, not all private schools are public schools).

Vocational learning

Education that provides practical training for a specific occupation or vocation; for example, agriculture, carpentry or beauty therapy. Traditionally this is delivered through 'hands-on' experience rather than academic learning, although there may be a combination of these elements depending on the course.

Assignments

Brainstorming

- In small groups, discuss what you know about education in the UK. Consider the following points:
    - What kinds of schools are there in the UK?
    - What exams do pupils have to sit in the UK?
    - What do you know about free schools and academies?

Research

- In pairs, brainstorm to find out what you know about the education system in Britain. How does it vary between England, Wales, Scotland and Ireland? What compulsory exams must pupils take and when?

- Do some research about the schools in your local area. Choose a school and investigate how it differs from your own – write some notes and feedback to your class.

- Find out about the differences between IGCSE, IBac and GCSE. Write some notes that explain your findings.

- Look at some education-based news stories from the last fortnight. What issues are currently being discussed and how would these affect you and your school? Write some notes and then discuss in small groups.

- Using the Internet, carry out research into the different types of schools available in Britain. How do you think a student's experience of school would differ in a comprehensive state school compared to a fee-paying independent school? Do you think the Government's recent introduction of 'free schools' is a good idea? Discuss your thoughts with a partner.

Design

- Design a poster that will raise awareness of exam stress and include some tips on how to manage it.

- Choose one of the articles in this topic and create an illustration to highlight the key themes/message of your chosen article.

- Design a leaflet that outlines the difference between IGCSE, A-levels and the International Baccalaureate.

- In groups, imagine that you have been given a government grant to start your own free school. Think of a name for your school and create a manifesto that details your ethos and aims. You could include drawings/plans of classrooms, sample logos or uniforms... get creative!

- In groups of four, design a large wall poster giving information on the different types of schools available.

Oral

- 'At four years old, children are far too young to sit exams.' Divide your class into two groups and stage a debate in which half of the class agrees with this statement, and half disagrees.

- Choose an illustration from this topic and, in pairs, discuss what you think the artist was trying to portray in this image.

- In small groups, discuss home education. Do you think that it is more suited to certain age groups? Consider the effect that it may have on GCSEs and A-levels. Would it be possible to study for all subjects without a qualified teacher?

- 'Boys GCSE results are often lower than that of girls. In small groups discuss this statement. Think of reasons why this may be true.

- As a class, discuss school uniform. Consider the following points:
    - Is the uniform expensive/reasonable?
    - Are the school rules strict enough/too strict?
    - Why do you think that wearing uniform is a good idea?

Reading/writing

- Find out about the difference between vocational and non-vocational subjects. Write a short summary of which subjects may be of use to you in your future career and why.

- Write a one-paragraph definition of exam stress.

- Write a short piece of prose entitled 'A day in the life of a A-level student...' Imagine how a student may feel during the lead up to exams, and the things they may do to help them revise. Would they be excited or nervous? What challenges might they face?

- Read the article 'Two-thirds of school heads have cut teachers to save money'. Write down some ideas on how your school could save or raise money.

- Read 'Is homework necessary or a pointless waste of time?' and write a letter to your headteacher with your thoughts about homework. Is the amount you receive suitable for your studies? Do you think that you should receive more homework such as they do in China?

Acknowledgements

The publisher is grateful for permission to reproduce the material in this book. While every care has been taken to trace and acknowledge copyright, the publisher tenders its apology for any accidental infringement or where copyright has proved untraceable. The publisher would be pleased to come to a suitable arrangement in any such case with the rightful owner.

Images

All images courtesy of iStock except pages 3, 9, 10, 26, 34, 36, 37: Unsplash, pages 6, 12, 13, 22, 27, 32: Pixabay, and pages 17, 18, 28, 31, 35, 38: Rawpixel.

Illustrations

Don Hatcher: pages 1 & 11. Simon Kneebone: pages 8 & 23. Angelo Madrid: pages 20 & 29.

Additional acknowledgements

With thanks to the Independence team: Shelley Baldry, Danielle Lobban, Jackie Staines and Jan Sunderland.

Tracy Biram

Cambridge, May 2019